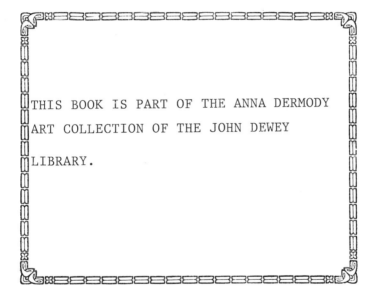

# *Gothic Illuminated Manuscripts*

# Gothic Illuminated Manuscripts

## Emma Pirani

# HAMLYN

Translated by Margaret Crosland from the Italian original

La miniatura gotica

© 1966 Fratelli Fabbri Editori, Milan

This edition © copyright 1970
THE HAMLYN PUBLISHING GROUP LIMITED
LONDON · NEW YORK · SYDNEY · TORONTO
Hamlyn House, Feltham, Middlesex, England

ISBN 0 600 01250 6

Text filmset by Filmtype Services, Scarborough, England

Printed in Italy by Fratelli Fabbri Editori, Milan

Bound in Scotland by Hunter and Foulis Ltd., Edinburgh

# Contents

# INTRODUCTION

For many centuries European art was heavily influenced by Byzantine art, which spread into the
territories of the Western Empire overrun by
Barbarians and provided a cultural norm for the civil
society which slowly emerged. Painting followed
Byzantine models very closely, as did the art of illumination, which is sometimes no more than a minor art
form used for decoration, but can often be fine art on a
small scale. Byzantine elements can be found in both
Carolingian and Romanesque work.

Towards the middle of the 13th century a new
spirit appeared in painting, which gradually underwent a transformation, as architecture had already
done. Artists turned from the Byzantine calligraphic
style, and in their search for a more direct image of
reality achieved effects of linear grace and harmony.
There is no clear line of demarcation between the
Romanesque and Gothic styles, for the changeover
was gradual, corresponding also to a transformation of
society affecting religion and philosophy, literary
culture and everyday customs. The advent of the
Gothic style was a European phenomenon, and it is
impossible to say whether its first meaningful expression in art occurred in France, England, Germany,
Venice, Lombardy or Florence.

# ITALY

## The Bolognese School

In Italy, the art of illumination reflected transalpine influences earlier than painting did, for the transport of codices was easier. The Gothic manner, which came from France, was superimposed on the Byzantine tradition; this had taken root in northern Italy, particularly in the Venetian states and Emilia, where it was kept alive by frequent contacts with the East. Padua and Bologna – particularly the latter – were the great centres of book production; this was linked with the universities, where the voluminous codices of civil and canon law were transcribed. Between the universities there were frequent exchanges, often for political reasons, of students and teachers, which also involved a retinue of probationers, assistants and illuminators. This meant that books produced in the two cities were similar in both calligraphy and illustrations, and it is easy to confuse them. For this reason there is some disagreement among critics about the epistolary by Giovanni da Gaibana, a liturgical codex in which are transcribed the Epistles read during Mass (plate 1). Some experts maintain that it was the work of an illuminator from Venezia, feeling that it is unlikely that such an intimate understanding of Byzantine forms existed outside the ambience of Venice; others have discerned in it a possible precursor of the Bolognese manner. Giovanni da Gaibana signs his name at the end of the codex, describing himself as a priest and scribe; those who have regarded him as both the scribe and the illuminator have related his place of origin – Gaibana, a small town in the duchy of Ferrara – to the style of the illumination, which is fairly close to that of Bologna. But whether or not he was the same person as the scribe, the artist who illustrated this codex possessed stronger links with Byzantine methods than Bolognese artists did; he adopted Byzantine techniques, using the same methods of handling colour 'and drapery. However, he rejected the ascetic abstraction of Byzantine art and attempted to give his figures weight. Every element of the picture shows the skill with which he adapted the imperial art of Byzantium to his purpose: the harmony and balance of the composition; the glitter of the gold backgrounds; the transparency of the colours, blue and red dominating and pinkish ochre, garnet red and pink melting into them in warm tonal harmony; and the iconography of the figures, some of which seem to have been derived from Roman models. The sense of movement and expressiveness of the figures, however, reveal a different, distinctively Western spirit. Current opinion is that the artist was Venetian, but the style closest to his is certainly that found in contemporary Bolognese illustrations of codices. In this city a favourable environment for book production had been created earlier than elsewhere, around the famous university which attracted scholars and teachers from all parts of Europe. Anyone who had completed his studies and was ready to

1   Epistolary by Giovanni da Gaibana. *The Entry into Jerusalem*. Biblioteca Capitolare, Padua.

**2** Psalter. MS. 346. Bolognese school. *The Entry into Jerusalem*. University Library, Bologna.

1    Epistolary by Giovanni da Gaibana. *The Entry into Jerusalem*. Biblioteca Capitolare, Padua. Splendid colours and harmonious compositions are found here along with stylised gestures and drapery; the solid, strong figures are still Romanesque in spirit.

2    Psalter. MS. 346. Bolognese school. *The Entry into Jerusalem*. University Library, Bologna. Comparison with the preceding illustration demonstrates that the Bolognese Gothic style, although inspired by Byzantine models, interpreted them in a new spirit.

3    Antiphonary. Cor. 16. Bolognese school. *Adoration of the Magi*. Museo Civico, Bologna. The Madonna enthroned, grave yet full of human feeling, is reminiscent of Cimabue; the expressiveness with which the three kings are rendered is emphasised by their almost identical attitudes and gestures.

4    Bible. MS. lat. 18. Bolognese school. Decorative roundel. Bibliothèque Nationale, Paris. The light, flowing veils worn by the dancer stand out against the intense colours of the background. The dark shadows used to emphasise her features are characteristic.

**3** Antiphonary. Cor. 16. Bolognese school. *Adoration of the Magi*. Museo Civico, Bologna.

4  Bible. MS. lat. 18. Bolognese school. Decorative
roundel. Bibliothèque Nationale, Paris.

return to his own country wanted to take with him a record of his work and some proof that his studies had been completed; he also needed the texts he had studied. The transcription was of course more accurate and more richly illustrated if the person who commissioned the work paid well for it. The volume of work was such as to bring prosperity to both the school of scribes and the many illuminators who worked in the bookshops or had their own schools.

The oldest of these schools had at first decorated religious texts, but later concentrated on the illustration of juridical codices. This was the school which followed the Byzantine tradition most closely; its art seems to have been directly inspired by the epistolary in plate 1. Contemporary with this is the illuminated work in the copy (1260) of the *Statue of the Threshers* (in Sta Maria della Vita, Bologna). The gentle Madonna on the first page is the first real example of the Bolognese style of illumination; the derivation of its colours and iconography from Byzantine work is quite clear. The affectionate gesture with which the mother clasps the child to her – he is not her Saviour but her child, clinging to her – is taken from Byzantine artists who, in the late 12th and the 13th century, sought to convey drama and emotion. But this work also has a grace and intensity comparable with Sienese painting, and this artist had evidently absorbed the teaching of Cimabue. A gradual in the Museo Civico, Bologna, (cor. 17) is certainly by a follower of Cimabue: the dramatic power of the master is particularly apparent in the pale St Francis about to receive the stigmata. He is kneeling in a bare landscape and raising his arms dramatically towards the Crucifixion, which has appeared in the sky. Other scenes used to decorate the large capital letters, for example a *Presentation in the Temple* and a *Vocation of Peter*, are closer to the Bolognese style. For this reason this codex is discussed with Bolognese work, although it is of Florentine origin; it demonstrates the reciprocal influences at work between the two cities.

The influence of Florentine art on that of Bologna is proved also in an antiphonary in the Museo Civico, Bologna (cor. 16). It is definitely Bolognese in execution. An *Adoration of the Magi* decorating a capital letter E (plate 3) has graceful and intensely expressive figures: although its derivation is Byzantine, the influence of Cimabue is unmistakeable. This influence is also present (though less obvious) in a psalter in the Biblioteca Universitaria, Bologna (MS 346). It is rich in colour with many illuminated paintings, each of which occupies a full page. The scenes invade the margins of the pages, and the characters of the narrative illustrated are fused harmoniously in form and colour with figurative elements of a geometrical, vegetable and animal type (plate 2). As in Venice and Padua, a new spirit enlivens the apparently Byzantine style of the codex. At first sight everything about it is Byzantine; the iconography, the technique, the traditional colours, the

gold backgrounds, the conventional shapes of mount-
ains. But in these crowded scenes, full of movement
and emotional force, there are reminiscences of the
great contemporary artists who were painting frescoes
on the walls of the finest churches in Italy – from
Cavallini to Giotto, from Duccio to Cimabue.

The manner is, however, a decidedly local one
indicative of the Bolognese school most closely
linked with the Byzantine tradition. The same school
that produced this psalter, and the antiphonary in the
Museo Civico, Bologna, produced some Bibles. They
are illustrated with gleaming gold leaf, and brilliant
and harmonious transparent colours, blue, pink, lilac,
red and grey, emphasised with white lead. There are
other examples, all quite similar, in the Bibliothèque
Nationale, Paris, as well as one in the British Museum
and one in Spain, at Gerona. There is a great deal of
ornamentation on every page: in the initial letters and
the margins and between the two columns of text;
with small figures of saints, angels, prophets, Christ
and the Madonna, either isolated or in scenes illustrating the Biblical text, following each other or
facing each other. They are often enclosed within
roundels which have blue and gold backgrounds or are
chequered in the French style; this seems to have been
derived from the stained-glass windows in French
churches (plate 4). The influence of French illumination can also be seen in the elegance of the small,
elongated and sinuous figures, and in the decoration in
the margins, where the leaf and flower motifs are inter-

**5** *Institutiones of Justinian*. MS. B. 18. Bolognese school. *The Emperor Justinian Enthroned*. Biblioteca Capitolare, Padua.

6  *Infortiatum of Justinian*. MS. S. IV. 2. Bolognese school.
*Viaticum for an invalid*. Biblioteca Malatestiana, Cesena.

5  *Institutiones of Justinian.* MS. B. 18. Bolognese school. *The Emperor Justinian Enthroned.* Biblioteca Capitolare, Padua. The static figures in this small gathering of people, to whom Justinian gives the law, possess weight and individuality; some of them are wearing the clothes of Bolognese lawyers, including the short ermine cloak.

6  *Infortiatum of Justinian.* MS. S. IV. 2. Bolognese school. *Viaticum for an invalid.* Biblioteca Malatestiana, Cesena. A scene full of movement, in which each figure expresses his individual feelings. The complexity of the scene may cause some confusion, but the artist has tried to present actions and people from everyday life.

7  Giovanni d'Andrea, *Novella in libros Decretalium.* MS. B. 42 inf. Niccolò da Bologna. *The Virtues and the Vices.* Biblioteca Ambrosiana, Milan. Some of the figures in this composition, for example Justice and Temperance, are among the strongest and most graceful that Niccolò produced.

8  Gratian, *Decretum.* MS. lat. 60. School of Niccolò da Bologna. University Library, Geneva. *Plea for divorce on the grounds of unconsummated marriage.* Salient episodes from a complicated case have been illustrated here. The rounded faces, with strongly, sometimes clumsily defined features, are typical of this school.

7   Giovanni d'Andrea, *Novella in libros Decretalium*. MS. B
42 inf. Niccolò da Bologna. *The Virtues and the Vices*.
Biblioteca Ambrosiana, Milan.

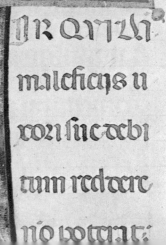

gr artili
malchisqs u
rō suctcbi
tum rcdctc
nō votrat:

woven with the strange and humorous figures of men and animals known as *drôleries*. These are fantastic hybrids, close to caricature, and allow the artist's imagination free rein.

The master who headed this school – of such artistic distinction and obviously connected with French art – was probably Oderisi, whom Dante called the master of the art 'which in Paris is called illumination'. Towards the end of the 13th century, however, 'the pages painted by Franco da Bologna are more cheerful' (Dante). It is impossible to characterise the work of Franco, of whom we know no more than we do of Oderisi: both are mentioned in documents and are famous only because Dante refers to them in the *Purgatorio*.

Dante's statement is supported by the change in the style of Bolognese illumination at the end of the 13th century. As the number of schools increased, they all tended to move away from the Byzantine tradition and record reality more directly, taking much from the contemporary schools of illumination in Paris. The change is gradual and can sometimes be detected within one codex, for example, one of the *Decretum* of Gratian, a collection of laws and cases of canonical law; it is in the Vatican Library (Vat. Lat. 1375).

An ability to create interesting illustrations to dry texts of civil and canonical law was a characteristic peculiar to the Bolognese illuminators, who constructed an iconography of their own for that purpose.

8    Gratian, *Decretum*. MS. lat. 60. School of Niccolò da Bologna. University Library, Geneva.

Displaying a lively narrative vein and introducing people and events from everyday life and civil and religious ceremonies, they provide a vivid picture of the customs of the period: doctors and scholars from the university, priests, popes, emperors, lords and ladies, artisans, peasants and soldiers, are shown in their characteristic dress.

The Vatican *Decretum* includes scenes illuminated by the same artist who had illustrated the Bibles now in Paris and London, and others which show a definite departure from the Byzantine style. The best of the other illustrators involved was probably Jacopino da Reggio, who added his signature at the end of the volume. The figures appear to be three-dimensional, movements occur within groups, and individual figures possess a life of their own; the harmony is no longer choral, but contrapuntal. The colours are more striking, sacrificing to realism the limpidity and harmoniousness of the Byzantine style. It is not certain whether the style of Franco is connected with this tendency; the striving for realism, and above all the decorative aspect of such work, expresses French Gothic themes by means of rough figures and harsh, muted colours.

It is more generally agreed that the influence of Franco's 'brush painting' is present in the two chorales in the Biblioteca Estense, Modena, (Q.1.4 and Q.1.1). Here the illumination reveals a delicate sense of colour and often achieves a broad pictorial effect. This illuminator had seen Cimabue's *Chorale* in the

Museo Civico, Bologna, and followed its iconography; his merits are the liveliness of his figures, his sense of composition, and the cheerful luminosity of his colours. For this reason some critics have preferred to see the manner of Franco in a third chorale in the Biblioteca Estense, Modena, the (R.1.6). The paint is more thickly impasted and the figures are stunted; what makes the work outstanding is its expressive vigour and the dramatic quality and vivacity of its composition. This artist had freed himself from Byzantine or French influences; the value given to the volumes makes it clear that he understood completely the innovations of Giotto.

These artists were probably still working between the end of the 13th and the early 14th century. A great many individuals and schools were active after them, in the first half of the 14th century. It is possible to differentiate between them but they have several more-or-less obvious characteristics in common: the importance they attach to volumes, the construction of well-modelled figures, and the inferiority of the colouring, which is often muted and watery, and not always harmonious. Examples are the *Decretum* in the Biblioteca Malatestiana, Cesena, (S.II.1) and the *Institutiones of Justinian* in the Biblioteca Capitolare, Padua, (plate 5), in which the figures are of a variety of types; some of them are decidedly crude, but they are given volume and individual characteristics.

Only towards the middle of the 14th century did Bolognese illumination free itself from the Franco-

**9** The Haberdashers' Certificate of 1328. No. 85. Bolognese school. *Madonna enthroned*. Museo Civiço, Bologna.

**10** Pope Gregory IX, *Decretales*. MS. lat. 3988. Bolognese school. *De accusationibus, inquisitionibus, denuntiabus*. Bibliothèque Nationale, Paris.

9   The Haberdashers' Certificate of 1328. No. 85. Bolognese school. *Madonna enthroned*. Museo Civico, Bologna. The mature technique of Bolognese illuminated work is evident in this rhythmic composition; strong colour and confident design produce a graceful effect.

10   Pope Gregory IX, *Decretales*. MS. lat. 3988. Bolognese school. *De accusationibus, inquisitionibus, denuntiabus*. Bibliothèque Nationale, Paris. The precision and naturalism of the figures, and the realistic architectural setting, make this one of the most mature examples of late 14th-century Bolognese illumination.

11   Seneca, *Tragoediae*. MS. C. 96 inf. School of Niccolò da Bologna. *Jason and Medea*. Biblioteca Ambrosiana, Milan. The classical text and the 'courtly' theme have prompted greater attention to detail and strong use of colour.

12   The Silk-weavers' Certificate of 1339. No. 86. Bolognese school. *Dealings in goods*. Museo Civico, Bologna. This pleasant scene is treated naturalistically; the figures have well-defined features and brightly coloured clothing.

13   *Officium B.M.V.* MS. 853. Bolognese school. *Threshing the grain (July)*. Biblioteca Comunale, Forlì. The anonymous illuminator who collaborated with a pupil of Niccolò da Bologna on this Little Office is clearly an artist of great skill; the harmony of the colouring, the balance of the composition and the accurate drawing of the figures in movement are outstanding.

**11**   Seneca, *Tragoediae*. MS. C. 96 inf. School of Niccolò da Bologna. *Jason and Medea*. Biblioteca Ambrosiana, Milan.

**12** The Silk-weavers' Certificate of 1339. No. 86. Bolognese school. *Dealings in goods*. Museo Civico, Bologna.

**13** *Officium B.M.V.* MS. 853. Bolognese school. *Threshing the grain (July)*. Biblioteca Comunale, Forli.

Byzantine tradition. Giotto's work became increasingly influential, and Bolognese painting also reached its apogee in these years, in the works of Vitale, Simone and Dalmasio. This liberation is mainly evident in the illuminations for juridical codices, literary works, and certificates and statutes of corporations, the iconography of which was less traditionally defined. The Haberdashers' Certificate of 1328 (Museo Civico, Bologna; no. 85) probably belongs to this period. The first page carries an illuminated painting of the Virgin (plate 9); this natural and graceful figure with almond-shaped eyes clearly derives from the Madonnas of contemporary Bolognese painting. The lower margin of the first page of the Drapers' Certificate of 1339 (Museo Civico, Bologna; no. 86) is decorated with a highly realistic scene in which two merchants display their wares to some clients who appear to be discussing their quality (plate 12).

The scenes which illustrate the juridical texts become progressively more animated. Several different incidents are often included in one picture, with a strong dramatic realism. The appearance and personality of individuals are emphasised more and more strongly, each expressing his own feelings; the scene acquires depth, though there are frequent errors in perspective. One interesting example can be found in a codex in the Biblioteca Malatestiana, Cesena. It contains the *Infortiatum* (plate 6), a collection of civil laws promulgated by Justinian which was one of the main texts used in studying law at Bologna. The figures of friars, doctors, matrons, young girls, nuns, ecclesiastics and children seem to have been taken from the urban life of Bologna; they are shown in the most varied attitudes, talking, weeping, praying, moving about or administering the sacraments. The buildings which constitute the background are no longer mere decorative elements in two dimensions, but acquire a depth of their own and dimensions in proportion to those of the figures.

This codex contains work somewhat similar in manner to that of an anonymous illuminator known as the Pseudo-Niccolò or, more frequently, The Illustrator. He was precise in his drawing and refined in his use of colour, reverting to the chromaticism of the Byzantine tradition. His style is similar to that of Niccolò di Giacomo; but his scenes have greater balance and in certain respects his early work anticipated that of Niccolò. The latter is probably the best known artist of the school which dominated Bolognese illumination during the second half of the 14th century, because he was the only Bolognese illuminator who signed his works. Paintings signed by him include some with figures of remarkable grace (especially those of women) with oval faces, slightly aquiline noses, small sensual mouths and long almond-shaped eyes. They derive from the figures painted by Niccolò's contemporary, Vitale degli Equi, the greatest Bolognese artist of this century.

Curiously enough, Niccolò also painted some crude

figures with large fleshy noses and low foreheads; they stand in contorted, often unrealistic attitudes, sometimes with absurd foreshortening. It is not clear whether this is the work of unskilled collaborators or represents an attempt by the master to characterise – and pass judgement on - certain types. Giovanni d'Andrea's *Commentary on the Decretals* in the Biblioteca Ambrosiana, Milan, (B.42 ing.) contains a picture (plate 7) with attractive little figures representing the virtues; at their feet, in contorted attitudes and with fleshy, vulgar faces, are the vices.

In many cases it is difficult to establish which illuminations were painted by Niccolò, which by his pupils or the Pseudo-Niccolò, and which by The Illustrator, a personality to whom most critics have attributed the best production of the school. The codices illustrated by this school are numerous, comprising religious, liturgical, literary and juridical texts. Among the latter are two containing the *Decretum* of Gratian. One is in the Bibliothèque Universitaire of Geneva (plate 8); in the other (State Library of Munich) the traditional iconography of the illustrations to the cases and judgements is enriched by the throng of bustling people. There is no lack of literary texts, such as the *Lucan* in the Biblioteca Trivulziana, Milan, and the *Tragedies* of Seneca in the Biblioteca Ambrosiana, Milan, (plate 11), which shows a particularly refined sense of colour. A Little Office in the Biblioteca Comunale, Forli, must also be mentioned (plate 13). Both the decoration and the figures are noticeably different from those of other codices illustrated by this school. The decoration surrounding the page is either entirely geometric or consists of a highly stylised leaf and flower pattern; it is enclosed by a coloured border in the Lombard manner. An illuminator who has been called Thomas of Modena was one of the artists who contributed to the illustrations; he constructed his figures with notable strength and balance, was a skilful colourist, and displays a feeling for nature akin to that found among the artists of Lombardy.

## The Florentine School

In Florence too, the first Gothic illuminations appeared during the second half of the 13th century; but they showed no clearly defined individual characteristics. Florentine work was dominated by the influence of Bolognese illumination; and this, as we have seen, was itself still strongly influenced by the Byzantine style. The teaching of the painters working in Florence was gradually disseminated nonetheless, as can be seen in some religious codices. In these, there are some figures clearly derived from the Byzantine manner of the Bolognese, and others whose design and proportions show the influence of the Florentine painters – of Coppo di Marcovaldo, for example, in some figures in a Gospel Book in the Biblioteca Nazionale, Florence (MS.II.I.167). Cimabue influenced illuminators more profoundly, as has already been pointed out. Florentine illuminators also imitated Cimabue, often freeing themselves from Bolognese influences; an example is reproduced in plate 14 – a Bible in the Biblioteca Laurenziana, Florence (MS. S.Croce Pl. V dext. 1).

At the beginning of the 14th century Florentine illumination began to show the effects of the revolution in painting begun by Giotto. His figures were too non-decorative to exercise an immediate and direct influence on illumination; the change was brought about by Giotto's students and by the general shift in taste caused by his work. The painter and illuminator Pacino di Bonaguida was a contemporary of Giotto; his *Tree of the Cross* (Galleria dell'Accademia, Florence) reveals his character as an illuminator, notably through the calligraphic details in Byzantine style which exist alongside figures modelled with volume and weight. Pacino is also thought to have illustrated the Bible (codex 2139) in the Biblioteca Trivulziana, Milan. In this there is a page (plate 18) illustrating the *Tree of the Cross* which is reminiscent of the work in the Accademia, Florence: it has the same exuberant decoration and the same grave figures, their treatment indicating Giotto's influence. Similar characteristics and qualities are present in some of the illuminations in the *Imagines vitae Christi* (Pierpont Morgan Library, New York), which represent scenes from the Bible and from the life of the Blessed Gerard of Germany. These are usually attributed (though not all experts agree with the attribution) to Pacino or his school; and the

14 *Old and New Testaments*. Plut. V, dext. I. Florentine school of the 13th century. *St James*. Biblioteca Laurenziana, Florence.

37

16   Domenico Lenzi, *The Corn Merchant*. MS. Tempi 3.
Florentine school of the 14th century. *The grain merchant*.
Biblioteca Laurenziana, Florence.

14   *Old and New Testaments.* Plut. V, dext. I. Florentine school of the 13th century. *St James.* Biblioteca Laurenziana, Florence. Byzantine influence is evident in the calligraphic treatment of the drapery in this illumination; the intense expressiveness of the face reveals the influence of Cimabue.

15   Domenico Lenzi, *The Corn Merchant.* MS. Tempi 3. Florentine school of the 14th century. Biblioteca Laurenziana, Florence. The style of this anonymous illuminator is derived from Florentine and Sienese painters. He illustrates in detail the vats full of grain, weighing-devices, and the merchant, who takes down the orders given by his client.

16   Domenico Lenzi, *The Corn Merchant.* MS. Tempi 3. Florentine school of the 14th century.. *The grain merchant.* Biblioteca Laurenziana, Florence. A pleasant impression of commercial activity — selling, making contracts and valuing — around the brimming containers of grain.

17   Zucchero Bencivenni, *The Pater Noster in the Vernacular.* MS. II, VI. 16. Florentine, 14th century. *Allegory of Sobriety.* Biblioteca Laurenziana, Florence. A figure of great elegance, enhanced by the great wings framing the head.

18   Bible. MS. 2139. Pacino di Bonaguida. *Crucifixion.* Biblioteca Trivulziana, Milan. This is a beautiful composition of great decorative exuberance, strengthened by the brightness of the colouring.

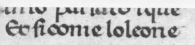

**17** Zucchero Bencivenni. *The Pater Noster in the Vernacular*. MS. II, VI. 16. Florentine, 14th century. *Allegory of Sobriety*. Biblioteca Laurenziana, Florence.

solidity of the figures and the rhythm of the composition represents the highest point of this master's art.

Another Florentine artist who, like Pacino, was influenced by Giotto – though his manner and outlook were quite different from Pacino's – was an anonymous painter known as the Master of St Cecilia, after his most characteristic work. This is an altar screen (now in the Uffizi), and indicates that he possessed the qualities of both illustrator and narrator. It is possible that none of the illuminations which seem to be related to this work were actually executed by him, but they were certainly from his school. The most interesting are those in the *Laudario* in the Biblioteca Nazionale, Florence (II.I.122). This codex is famous for both its rich illustration and the music contained in it; it is a basic document in the history of Italian music. It is extremely rich in illuminated work which has been attributed to various artists. One, in the Sienese manner, resembles the work of Pietro Lorenzetti; another derives from the manner of Neri of Rimini, the head of a school of illustrators in Rimini. (The school was active for a few years at the beginning of the 14th century, working in an unmistakably Giottesque style). The most recent writer on this subject, Salmi, recognises Sienese characteristics in some of the illustrations in this codex, but definitely ascribes the work itself to the Florentine school. He identifies some illustrations as deriving from Pacino; in other parts of the codex he believes

18   Bible. MS. 2139. Pacino di Bonaguida. *Crucifixion*.
Biblioteca Trivulziana, Milan.

the influence of the Master of St Cecilia to be stronger. This can be seen, for example, in a delicate, hieratic choir of angels, the thin cold colours of whose clothing and wings stand out against the intense blue of the sky. The illuminator most strongly influenced by Sienese work is the painter of the intensely expressive *Noli me tangere* in plate 21. The delicate, flowing design is inserted harmoniously into the initial O, and the way in which the figure of Christ follows the curve of the letter creates a surprising effect of pathos. The dark colours indicate the Florentine origin of the illumination. The rest of the work is in the Sienese manner, frequently used by Florentine illuminators at this time, since its delicacy and grace was particularly well-suited to the illustration of codices.

This does not mean that Florentine painters like Orcagna, or such earlier artists as Bernardo Daddi, who resembled Giotto more directly, were uninfluential. Something of Daddi's influence can be seen, for example, in a codex in the Biblioteca Laurenziana, Florence. This is known as *Il Biadaiolo* (The Corn Merchant) (MS. Tempi 3) because the corn merchant, Domenico Lenzi, registered the prices of Florentine cereals between 1320 and 1335 in it. It also contains moral considerations and historical notes. The codex is richly and entertainingly illustrated: 'there are many full-page scenes of Florentine life, for example of the market of Orsanmichele and its gates, through which the citizens go to distribute alms to the poor. Indoor scenes are shown with a wealth of detail: in the grain merchant's crowded shop (plate 15) the merchant is writing down the prices while talking to a client. The work shows the influence of Florentine followers of Giotto, and of some Sienese painters, in particular Ambrogio Lorenzetti, whose *Good and Bad Government* frescos convey the atmosphere of life in Siena.

Elements of Bernardo Daddi's manner, enlivened by Sienese colouring, are more clearly discernible in two codices in the Biblioteca Laurenziana, Florence: an *Antiphonarum diurnum* (cor. 41) and a missal (MS. Edili 107). Both are illustrated by the same artist, whose scenes reveal a lively feeling for the picturesque; both include scenes crowded with people realistically grouped in landscapes. The spatial treatment of the figures endows the illuminations with something of the power of frescoes. This can be seen in the painting of St Frediano diverting the waters of the Serchio from the walls of the city, and even more clearly in the miracle of St Zanobius (c. 367 r. of the missal), in which the crowd is admirably rendered. This monumental quality also appears in minor scenes, inside the large initial letters of the antiphonary or variously arranged throughout the pages of the missal. Round the pages run subtle, delicately coloured designs with small and elegant human figures or animals (plates 22 and 23).

The painter Jacopo da Casentino, who was active during the second quarter of the 14th century, was also an illuminator. In Salmi's opinion, Jacopo was

**19** *Missale Romanum*. Jacopo da Casentino (?) *Presentation in the Temple*. Seminario del Cestello, Florence.

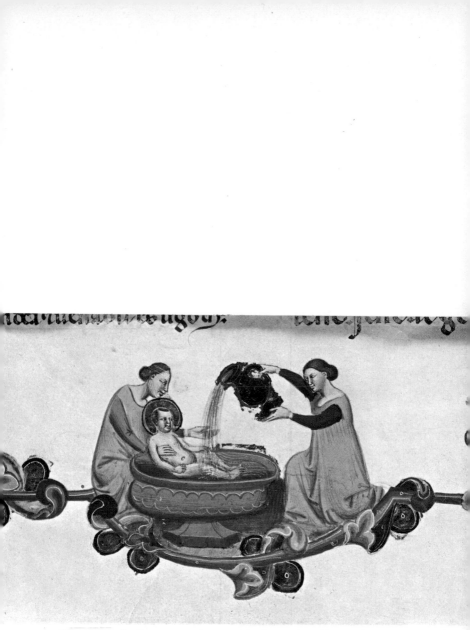

20  *Missale Romanum*. Jacopo da Casentino (?) *Nativity of the Virgin* (detail). Seminario del Cestello, Florence.

19 *Missale Romanum*. Jacopo da Casentino (?) *Presentation in the Temple*. Seminario del Cestello, Florence. These intense figures, painted by Jacopo or one of his pupils, are rendered in the manner of Giotto's followers in Florence. There is something particularly expressive about the figure of the aged Simeon, and the affectionate gesture with which he bends over to welcome the slightly frightened child.

20 *Missale Romanum*. Jacopo da Casentino (?) *Nativity of the Virgin* (detail). Seminario del Cestello, Florence. There is a feeling of intimate family happiness about the bathing of the new-born baby. The scene is harmoniously integrated into the design; the volute is balanced by the angel's gesture as he pours out the water.

21 *Laudario*. MS. II.I. 122. Florentine illumination. *Noli me tangere*. Biblioteca Nazionale, Florence. The flowing lines of the composition indicate a Sienese origin. Mary Magdalene's attitude is one of passionate and fearful devotion.

22 *Antiphonarium Diurnum*. Cor. 41. Florentine, school of Daddi. *Assumption of the Virgin*. Biblioteca Laurenziana, Florence. The intense spirituality of the scene, extending beyond the capital with a powerful sense of movement, is in complete harmony with the decorative refinement of the painting; notice the elegant gesture with which St Dominic reaches up to take the girdle from the Virgin Mary.

21 *Laudario*. MS. II.I. 122. Florentine illumination. *Noli me tangere*. Biblioteca Nazionale, Florence.

48

anz cuch
ll dulcrosc

óff. Beata es uirgo maria,

22 *Antiphonarium Diurnum*. Cor. 41. Florentine, school of
Daddi. *Assumption of the Virgin*. Biblioteca Laurenziana,
Florence.

responsible for some of the illuminations in an antiphonary in the Biblioteca Comunale in Poppi, his
birthplace. He introduced into illuminated work his
own Giottesque pictorial style, derived from Bernardo
Daddi and Taddeo Gaddi. He and his school are
believed to have illustrated such codices as the
*Precepts of the Ancients* by Bartolomeo da S. Concordia
(Pal. 600 in the Biblioteca Nazionale, Florence) and a
missal in the Seminario del Cestello, Florence; in
this Jacopo collaborated with an anonymous painter
called the Master of the Dominican Effigies. The
missal, which is particularly richly decorated, is
embellished with numerous initials containing scenes
and figures; these extend beyond the area of the
initial and invade the margins, mingling with the
elegant motifs of the border. Some of the sacred
scenes on the borders complement those within the
initial letters. In the initial on c. 255 r. for example, the
*Birth of the Virgin Mary* is represented, and in the
lower margin, inserted in the border, is a scene
showing the new-born child being washed (plate 20).
The same feeling for colour and composition can be
observed in the scenes inside the initials, for example
the *Presentation in the Temple* in plate 19; the figures
have, besides, a restrained expressive intensity.

The influence of Florentine painters also appears in
the figures illustrating the *Pater Noster in the Vernacular* by Zucchero Bencivenni (Biblioteca Nazionale,
Florence; MS. II.VI.16). This is dated 1379 and was
executed by several artists. Among the most interesting

illuminations is the *Allegory of Sobriety* (plate 17), which has great linear and rhythmical elegance, and bright colours. Some authorities believe that it was influenced by the frescos of Andrea da Firenze, who painted the great allegorical cycles in the Spanish Chapel of Sta Maria Novella, Florence.

The most active and clearly defined school of Florentine illuminators was that of the Camaldo monastery of Sta Maria degli Angeli; in the 15th century it was an extremely important seat of humanistic studies. The most active and best-known member of the school was Simone of Siena, also called Simone Camaldolese; but there were probably Camaldolese illuminators before him who achieved expressive power and refinement in the handling of pictorial and decorative elements. Between 1370 and 1377 several artists illustrated a gradual (plates 24 and 26) now in the Biblioteca Laurenziana, Florence, (cor. 2); but there is one whose work displays a particular intensity. It is evidently based on the teaching of contemporary Florence painters (Nardo and Andrea di Dione in particular), and achieves effects of composition and luminosity which foreshadow Lorenzo Monaco.

The first codex signed and dated by Simone da Siena is an *Antiphonary from Advent to Easter* of 1381 in the Biblioteca Laurenziana (cor. 39). It was in this year that Simone took his vows at the monastery of Sta Maria degli Angeli. There are codices illuminated by him or his collaborators in other places than the Biblioteca Laurenziana: the monastery of S. Pancrazio, Vallombrosa, the Sacristy of Sta Croce, the Museum of St Mark's and the convent of Il Carmine, Florence, and the Museo Civico, Bologna. Simone's activity has been compared to that of Niccolò da Bologna, for a large number of codices by him have been preserved – a fact that proves his popularity with contemporaries. Although he came from Siena, whose art had reached its apogee in the first half of the century, he remained faithful to Florentine taste, deriving his style from the school of Orcagna. His compositions are skilfully balanced and his colouring is bright; his figures are modelled on ample lines with constructive vigour. The dense, ostentatious decoration around the pages and on initial letters is extremely rich: the thin, delicate stems, like branches in spring, painted by artists of the preceding generation, are now covered with an abundance of leaves and bright, fleshy flowers. Simone often signed his works, for example the *Nativity* in a large initial H in an antiphonary in Sta Croce, Florence, (cod. B). The whole page is an instance of his decorative style, and is also outstanding as a graphic composition. Even when his works are not signed his manner is easily recognisable by the harmonious composition, the gravity and weight of the figures, and the exuberance of the decoration. An example is the luminously coloured *Annunciation* within a large initial R in an antiphonary carried out for the monastery of S. Pancrazio (Biblioteca Laurenziana, cor 40).

The work of Lorenzo Monaco, the greatest

representative of the school of Sta Maria degli Angeli, brings us to the threshold of the 15th century and the Renaissance, although his style should still be defined as late Gothic. Like Simone, he was a Sienese, and he entered Sta Maria degli Angeli exactly ten years later than Simone. His style was largely formed by study of the paintings of the Orcagna brothers. The refined colouring and spiritual quality of his figures, with their hollow and intense faces, gives his art a poetic and profoundly religious content. He had the Sienese sense of colour and love of decorative composition, which he also displayed in the richness of his floral designs. Among the first expressions of his art are some initial letters in an antiphonary preserved in the Biblioteca Laurenziana (cor. 5) which already shows all his vigour (plate 25).

Lorenzo illuminated many codices and had many followers, including Bartolomeo da Fruosino who was a pupil of Agnolo Gaddi. The slender elegance of Fruosino's figures is in fact derived from Gaddi; but the composition of pages like the one from the *Antiphonary of Sta Maria Nuova*, now in the Museum of St Mark's, Venice, shows how close Fruosino came to the decorative taste of Lorenzo.

## The Sienese School

Other schools flourished in Tuscany, Pisa and Siena. The Sienese school produced many works and won great fame because of the individual sense of colour and decoration shown by Sienese artists. The

Innat sā iohis

matris mee uocauit me

**23** *Missale Romanum.* MS. Edili 107. Florentine, school of Daddi. *Nativity of St John the Baptist.* Biblioteca Laurenziana, Florence.

23   *Missale Romanum.* MS. Edili 107. Florentine, school of Daddi. *Nativity of St John the Baptist.* Biblioteca Laurenziana, Florence. The depth of the picture and the monumental quality of the figures demonstrate the extent to which the artist had absorbed the innovations of Giotto; his little scenes have the impact of frescos.

24   Gradual. Cor. 2. School of Sta Maria degli Angeli. *St Lucy.* Biblioteca Laurenziana, Florence. This figure has been skilfully constructed, and the colouring is intensely luminous. The master responsible for it, although still influenced by the style of Daddi, is a precursor of the art of Lorenzo Monaco.

25   Antiphonary. Cor. 5. Lorenzo Monaco. *St Michael the Archangel.* Biblioteca Laurenziana, Florence. The use of colour and drawing derive from Orcagna; and the figure is extremely elegant.

26   Gradual. Cor. 2. School of Sta Maria degli Angeli. *St Philip and St James.* Biblioteca Laurenziana, Florence. This is the work of the master who painted the *St Lucy.* He has given the two saints the same gentle quality and diaphanous luminosity.

**24**   Gradual. Cor. 2. School of Sta Maria degil Angeli. *St Lucy.* Biblioteca Laurenziana, Florence.

57

**25** Antiphonary. Cor. 5. Lorenzo Monaco. *St Michael the Archangel*. Biblioteca Laurenziana, Florence.

26   Gradual. Cor. 2. School of Sta Maria degli Angeli. *St Philip and St James*. Biblioteca Laurenziana, Florence.

early productions of the school (13th century) were strongly Byzantine-Bolognese in style; but the highly individual interpretation of Byzantinism by Sienese painters from Duccio to Simone Martini and the Lorenzetti quickly brought about a change. As Petrarch testifies, it was Simone Martini himself who introduced his art onto the pages of the codices during his stay at the Papal Court in Avignon; and his famous *Virgil* (Biblioteca Ambrosiana, Milan; A.49 inf.) interprets a humanistic conceit suggested by Petrarch himself. But the colour and sinuousness of the Gothic line was brought to the Sienese codex mainly by pupils of the great painters – from Memmo di Filipuccio, who interpreted the Sienese-Byzantine style with forms like those of Duccio, to Lippo Vani, who designed his figures on ample lines derived from the Lorenzetti. But the high point of Sienese illumination is perhaps the *Codex of St George* by the anonymous pupil of Simone Martini. It was executed at Avignon in about 1340, and is now in the Chapter Library of St Peter's, Vatican City (MS. C.120). The codex contains a history of the miracles and martyrdom of Saint George, written by Cardinal Jacopo Stefaneschi, who lived in Avignon at the time. The scenes are freely composed with a fresh narrative vein, and the figures are harmonious. Apart from the influence of the master, Simone Martini, this artist had obviously felt the charm of French courtly illumination, on which he in turn probably exerted some influence.

## The Venetian School

In the Venetian states, as in Tuscany, the art of illumination underwent Bolognese influence in the second half of the 13th century. This influence was also strongly felt in Padua, illuminators from Bologna working there close to the university. The epistolary of 1259 remained an isolated masterpiece, grouped with the Benedictine missal of Admond in Styria and the Gospel Book now in the Fitzwilliam Museum, Cambridge; they are all attributed to the same artist, who came from either Padua or Venice. Only this artist's Bolognese contemporaries knew how to interpret the strictly Byzantine tradition in a spirit of subtle and refined innovation.

The courtly Byzantine tradition was interpreted in a very different spirit in Venice. In one of the illustrations to the *Descriptio Terrae Sanctae* by Burchardus Theutonicus, the city of Jerusalem (plate 29) is painted against a gold background, constructed with harmonious lines and striking colours; two lines of horsemen are advancing into this city while other warriors defend it from the top of the walls. The figures are insubstantial, and their function could be described as principally decorative; indeed, the whole composition lacks narrative feeling, which has been sacrificed to linear harmony of the Byzantine type. Only the decorative motifs on the border show a hint of the Gothic.

Byzantine linearism also appears in the early 14th-century *Leggendario* in the Vatican Library (Vat. Lat.

27   Missal. MS. III. 111. Venetian. *Madonna and Saints*.
Biblioteca Marciana, Venice.

28   Missal. MS. III. 111. Venetian. *The Crucifixion of St Andrew*. Biblioteca Marciana, Venice.

27    Missal. MS. III. 111. Venetian. *Madonna and Saints.*
Biblioteca Marciana, Venice. The Bolognese manner of
interpreting the Byzantine style is still discernible in the
strict symmetry of this composition; but it is tempered by
softer outlines and the warm colours that seem to derive
from Paolo Veneziano.

28.    Missal. MS. III. 111. Venetian. *The Crucifixion of St
Andrew.* Biblioteca Marciana, Venice. The figures in this
composition, which belongs to the same codex as the Madonna
in plate 27, show the influence of Bolognese illumination more
strongly. The scene is dominated by the powerful figure of the
saint.

29    Burchardus Theutonicus, *Descriptio Terrae Sanctae.* MS.
74. Venetian. *The Siege of Jerusalem.* Biblioteca del Seminario, Padua. This splendid design is executed in brilliant
Byzantine colouring; the slender and insubstantial figures of
the warriors, on the other hand, have a Gothic air.

29    Burchadus Theutonicus, *Descriptio Terrae Santae.* MS.
74. Venetian. *The Siege of Jerusalem.* Biblioteca del Seminario, Padua.

375), though it is a quality more typical of the Byzantine revival of the 12th-13th centuries. The artist who illustrated this work created vibrant, dramatic figures and infused some scenes with a sense of movement close to the Gothic spirit. On the other hand, elements reminiscent of the popular aspect of Bolognese taste appear in the Gospel Book in the Biblioteca Marciana, Venice, (MS. lat. I. 100) and the missal in the same collection (MS. lat. III. 111). They are more evident in the Gospel Book; the decoration on some pages recalls that of the psalter in the Biblioteca Universitaria of Bologna. The missal is illustrated by several artists, including one similar to the artist who illustrated certain Hungarian codices of Bolognese origin; another contributor is more sensitive to the Byzantine tradition, though it is the tradition as interpreted in the teachings of such Venetian painters as Paolo Veneziano (plates 27 and 28).

This painter's style can be seen more clearly, and with better colouring, in some *Mariegolas* in the Museo Correr, Venice. Despite the monumentality of the figures, the painter displays a tendency to follow Byzantine models which is particularly evident in the rigid calligraphy of the drapery. About the same time (1365) an artist from the Emilia, Giustino di Gherardino from Forlì, was working in Venice. Certain of his colouring techniques in the gradual he illustrated for the Scuola di Sta Maria della Carità (Biblioteca Marciana, Venice, lat. II. 119) demonstrate that he had brought Emilian techniques with him to Venice. In a group of friars in white robes, for example (plate 33), the tonal delicacy of the painting and the graceful attitudes of the kneeling figures against a gold background are far from the spirit of Niccolò da Bologna and his school (which was active in Bologna at this time); in fact it is more like certain delicate French Gothic works.

The characteristics of Venetian illuminated work appear in the illustrations to the *Entrée d'Espagne* in the Biblioteca Marciana (MS. fre. 21/25); They were certainly carried out by artists from the Veneto, if not from Venice itself. The codex, which comes from the Biblioteca dei Gonzaga, was probably produced in Mantua, and reflects the artistic climate of this city where artists from Lombardy, the Venetian states and the Emilia all met. Richly illustrated on almost every page, the codex is an example of the style of illustration used in chivalric romances, which had multiplied in the court libraries of northern Italy from the end of the 13th century. The illumination was carried out at different periods and by different hands: at least three – more, according to Toesca, who believed that the illuminations ranged from the first decades to the second half of the 14th century. The artist who illustrated the early pages of the poem used little modelling and flat colours, but worked with spontaneity. The next draws his figures with a pen and colours them thinly with aquatint; he illustrated the text with duelling scenes (plate 30) which become monotonous through frequent repetition, though taken singly they are elegant and spirited. The third illuminator, who was working in the second half of the 14th century, is far superior: his technique is more refined and he achieves exciting pictorial effects. His compositions are full of knights on horseback besieging cities, confronting each other in closed ranks, drawn up beneath multicoloured fluttering standards, or engaged in battle (plate 31). The variety of themes he handles proves his complete liberation from the Byzantine tradition; his work is more reminiscent of Lombard, and occasionally Bolognese styles, though they are always interpreted in a purely personal way.

Towards the end of the century, illuminators became increasingly aware of the works of the major Venetian painters. The *Liber de principibus Carrariensibus* attributed to Vergerio (Museo Civico, Padua; MS. B.P.158) is illustrated with strong portraits of the Carrara princes vividly characterised. According to Toesca, they are based on the frescos (now lost) which Avanzo and Guariento painted in a room in the Carrara Palace. The influence of Altichiero appears in *De viris illustribus* by Petrarch, which was once in the Carrara Library and is now in the Bibliothèque Nationale in Paris (MS. lat. 6069 F). The manner of Giusto de'Menabuoi influenced the illuminator of the *Chronica de Carrariensibus* (Biblioteca Marciana, MS. lat. II 381), especially in certain crowded compositions like the one (plate 32) in which a member of the Carrara family, surrounded by gentlemen, is receiving the standard of the city. The figures are characterised but are slightly uneasy; the composition as a whole is tranquil, however, because of its warm colour harmony. The art of the Veronese and Paduan painters had some influence on the expressionistic manner of the masters who illustrated a codex of Dante's *Divine Comedy* (plate 34) now in the Biblioteca Marciana (MS. IX. 276). This is one of the most lavishly illustrated manuscripts of the poem, with one or more illuminations to each page; several different hands can be recognised, but the styles are homogeneous and are probably those of a master and his assistants.

To the same Paduan-Veronese school can be attributed the illumination of a *Biblia Historialis* in the Biblioteca dell'Accademia dei Concordi, Rovigo (MS. 212). In this Toesca has identified the hand 'of a mediocre illuminator between Guariento and Giusto de'Menabuoi', and Salmi noticed in a more general way some belated influence of Giotto. This relic of earlier art is also of great interest because it is perhaps the unique example of a *Biblia Historialis*; that is, a Bible with narrative illustrations and a commentary consisting only of a short explanatory text in which the incident is narrated in the vernacular. (In this case, one of the Venetian dialects). The Rovigo volume contains only a fragment of the Bible (Genesis and the Book of Ruth); there are 344 illustrations, four to a page. They comprise an exceptional series

Que ſes paroles ꝶ ſes diz côptm.
Car les nuf ꝓz larôs lo proua.
Entres dos lers encros le adaua.
Roľ. ioi apue ne forſena.
Il done un ſaut elebrûz enteſa.
Tient dûndurt que nâgiez ſequndi.
Mais le pnes ſon fuſt lui pſentu.
Voit le .Roľ. dumetiex reclama.
Contre leſuſt qe ſoz lui deuala.
Alerenere le brât diciei gita.
Paz ſignât force qe tot reâtina.
Entre deus barés le tinel enconnt.

Paz deus moiteez le trére ꝶ de copa.
Le tnochôs chiet tôt tot ſe côforta.
Le mes Carlos emôroie cria.
Qe la uertu qe nrê ſtz môſtra.
Acelui ſpit dottinât meraia.
Dât . Fenagu uoit tot ſon tinel.
Trunaie paz mi ans nil ualdret êrtel.
Remiſt plaiſ one ôduel edercuel.

**30**   *Entrée d'Espagne*. MS. fr. 21 (25). Venetian. *A Duel.*
Biblioteca Marciana, Venice.

31  *Entrée d'Espagne*. MS. fr. 21 (25). Venetian. *Siege of a City*. Biblioteca Marciana, Venice.

30 *Entrée d'Espagne.* MS. fr. 21 (25). Venetian. *A Duel.* Biblioteca Marciana, Venice. One of many similar scenes by this artist; although the composition is not particularly original, it displays a certain acuteness of observation.

31 *Entrée d'Espagne.* MS. fr. 21 (25). Venetian. *Siege of a City.* Biblioteca Marciana, Venice. Although this scene belongs .to the same codex as the preceding illustration, it is by an artist who worked a good deal later, using thick, bright colouring with striking vigour.

32 *Chronica de Carrariensibus.* MS. lat. X. 381. Venetian. *The Handing-over of the City Standard to a member of the Carrara family.* The warm colouring and dense crowd of applauding citizens confer gaiety and vitality on this scene, albeit the individual figures are somewhat rigid and inexpressive.

**32** *Chronica de Carrariensibus*. MS. lat. X. 381. Venetian. *The Handing-over of the City Standard to a member of the Carrara family.*

of pictures of daily life: country scenes (harvests among ripening corn, pastoral scenes), scenes of town life and scenes of interiors (banquets, costumes of various colours). Several artists of widely different skill can be distinguished, but they all derive to a greater or lesser extent from Giotto. The best of them produces notably well-modelled figures, often a little thick-set but always moving naturally and well placed in a landscape or interior with adequate depth. The influence of Giotto is evident in the breadth of the figures, and in certain of their attitudes: Ruth spinning in front of her house, for example, recalls the girl in the *Annunciation* in the Scrovegni chapel. In the scene of the *Blessing of Jacob* (plate 35) Rebecca listening at the door of Isaac's bedroom recalls the girl trying to see-and-yet-not-see the meeting between Joachim and Anna, hiding behind the city gate but leaning out to look. The figures are well-constructed and the narration is pleasing and realistic, though it lacks the expressive intensity of Giotto and his school.

The illustrations to the *Registrum omnium possessionum* (convent of Sta Mattia, Murano) exhibit a similar narrative quality, but reality is represented with more immediacy and subtlety; the single figures are strongly characterised, like portraits drawn during a discussion. The illuminator, who was also an innovator in the way he used ornamental motifs, belonged to the circle of Cristoforo Cortese, but according to Toesca and Pallucchini was at work earlier. There is an illumination by Cristoforo, signed on some detached pages from the *Mariegola* in the Scuola di Misericordia, in the Wildenstein Collection in New York. A large initial F contains a scene showing the funeral of Saint Francis; it is crowded with friars and angels against a background with arabesques of the type painted by Niccolò da Bologna. After living for some time in Bologna, Cristoforo had been influenced by the teaching of the Bolognese school there; but although he also remained faithful to certain Gothic modules, it is quite clear that he was fascinated by the Venetian painters working in the late 14th and early 15th century, when Gentile da Fabriano was already active. The work of Cristoforo is thus transitional, bridging the Gothic and Renaissance styles.

*The Lombard School*
Gothic illumination in Lombardy was not exempt from Bolognese influences, although they were not as strong in other regions of Italy. There is a considerable distance between Bolognese taste and the illuminations for the '*From the New and the Old Testament*', stories narrated by Pietro Bescarpe in a little poem in Milanese dialect (Biblioteca Braidense, Milan; AD XIII 48). The illuminations are of a popular nature, graceful and expressive, with flat colouring. They demonstrate that by the middle of the 13th century – the codex is dated 1264 – the influence of French Gothic had been superimposed on the traditional

Byzantine styles; French models had probably reached Lombardy together with the chivalric poems so much appreciated and sought after at the courts of northern Italy, where they were transcribed and illustrated. Examples of Lombard illumination at this period are too rare to permit more definite statements. Besides, Lombard work did not become clearly individuated until the first decades of the 14th century.

Of outstanding interest are the illustrations to the *Liber Pantheon* by Goffredo da Viterbo, one of the most prized and discussed codices of the 14th century. Some experts have attributed them to a Bolognese illuminator; others claim that they possess characteristics peculiar to Lombardy. Written in Milan in 1331 and dedicated to Azzone Visconti, the codex is profusely illuminated with lively scenes inserted among the lines of the text, continuing the narrative in the margins with greater freedom of compostion. It is now in the Bibliothèque Nationale, Paris (MS. lat. 4895).

The existence of other codices with illuminations comparable to those of the *Liber Pantheon*, for example a *Passionario* in the Biblioteca Ambrosiana (MS. P.165 sup.), has made it possible to posit the existence of an entire school of Bolognese illuminators resident in Milan, or of Lombards trained at the school of Bologna.

Remote from Bolognese taste and closer to French Gothic are the illustrations for a chivalric romance,

**33** Gradual. MS. lat. II, 119. Giustino di Gherardino of Forlì, *Brothers of the School of Sta Maria della Carità worshipping the Virgin*. Biblioteca Marciana, Venice.

33   Gradual. MS. lat. II. 119. Giustino di Gherardino of Forlì. *Brothers of the School of Sta Maria della Carità worshipping the Virgin.* Biblioteca Marciana, Venice. Within the initial letter a group of friars worship the Virgin, who appears in the sky; in the lower margin they worship her image with great fervour inside a church. This composition is characterised above all by its luminous and refined tonality.

34   Dante, *Divine Comedy.* MS. IX. 276. Paduan-Veronese school. *Dante and Beatrice before Justinian.* Biblioteca Marciana, Venice. This is one of the strongest and most pertinent illustrations of Dante's *Paradiso.* The Lombard style of the illuminator has been considerably modified by elements taken from Veronese painters.

35   *Biblia Historialis.* MS. 212. Paduan-Veronese school. *Isaac blessing Jacob.* Biblioteca dell'Accademia dei Concordi, Rovigo. A careful and detailed realistic study with reminiscences of Giotto; the head and face of Isaac are treated with great realism.

34   Dante, *Divine Comedy*. MS. IX. 276. Paduan-Veronese school. *Dante and Beatrice before Justinian*. Biblioteca Marciana, Venice.

the *Tristan*, transcribed at the Court of the Visconti, probably during the first decades of the century (Bibliothèque Nationale, Paris; MS. fr. 755). In this the originality and refinement of Lombard illumination is revealed by a succession of scenes from court life in Milan: the duke receiving a warrior's homage; a banquet for courtiers: subjects doing homage to the duke and his wife against a background of Gothic palaces in which the style of the castle of Pavia is repeated. There are also extremely lively hunting scenes (plate 37), duels and battles, which are never allowed to become monotonous. The figures are rendered with delicate lines, and their outstanding dramatic quality and brilliant colouring are delightfully appropriate to the world of fable.

In the second half of the century, the influence of the Visconti court became increasingly strong. As a result, Lombard illuminators were much occupied in decorating codices for the library in the castle of Pavia or for the aristocracy. At this time Milan, under the leadership of Gian Galeazzo Visconti, continued to extend its frontiers. Contact with transalpine Gothic art was further stimulated by interest in romance literature; hence Provençal troubadours and chivalric poems were imported. Conversely, the Visconti court attracted French artists, who flocked there in especially large numbers towards the end of the century to work on the Cathedral. The 'courtly' atmosphere also explains the particular type of works illustrated, and the courtly style of the illustrations. Contact with French art, occurring more frequently than in other regions of Italy, was responsible for the particular style which developed in Lombardy: a style which certainly displayed individual characteristics but indisputably reflects the influence of French Gothic.

A number of strongly-marked personalities dominate Lombard illumination of the late 14th century. Some are known by name; others are identified by the name of the most important codex they illuminated. Examples are the Master of the *Book of Hours of Isabella of Castile* and the Master of the *Vitae Imperatorum*. Some of the codices were devotional works for the use of members of the ducal family – Little Offices or Books of Hours containing the prayers to be recited during the various religious offices and those for the various hours of the day. Others were liturgical codices richly decorated for the duke to present to a church or monastery. More often the codices were secular – chivalric romances, classical texts and histories (though these became very popular only from the beginning of the 15th century, when the Humanist spirit was becoming widespread). The Visconti Library contained many works of a scientific nature, notably the *Tacuinum Sanitatis*, a manual of hygiene dealing with the quality of food and drink and the effect of the seasons on the constitution and behaviour of men. This provided an opportunity for lively scenes of town and country life. All the figures are elegant, whether they be saints, ladies or courtiers; and the scenes are full of animals, which the Visconti loved. Coats of arms and ducal emblems also abound, either within the decoration or else forming separate decorative motifs. The work is a visual counterpart of Gualvano Fiamma's descriptions of Milan in his chronicle. He describes the splendours of the chapel (S. Gottardo) and palace built for Azzo Visconti after 1335: the 'amphitheatres' with birds and wild animals (lions, bears, monkeys and baboons), the frescos with figures of Aeneas, Attila, Charlemagne and Azzo himself, the fountains with fish, the gardens, the little lakes. And he records the fashions adopted after 1340: the men wear short, foppish tunics and ride at full tilt through the city, the ladies wear low cut gowns of multicoloured silk interwoven with gold and adorned with jewels.

The first illuminator of this period known by name is Giovanni di Benedetto da Como, who signed a Book of Hours for Blanche of Savoy, the wife of Galeazzo Visconti II (State Library, Munich; MS. lat. 23215). The figures are well drawn, and are placed in natural attitudes against backgrounds of Gothic architecture, supported – as in the scene of the Annunciation – by slender columns; on the chequered backgrounds brilliant gold alternates with bright colours. The same artist is usually credited with the very similar Book of Hours in the Biblioteca Estense, Modena (S.2.31).

The illuminator of *Guiron le Courtois* was a better

artist. The illustrations to this chivalric romance follow the narrative step by step with acute observation of nature and minute attention to detail. They cover the lower margins on each page, the side margins and the space between two columns of text, so that the text often looks as if it has been pasted on to the picture (plate 36). There are conversations inside and outside buildings which are drawn with architectural precision and a sense of volume which gives depth to the space. King Arthur is shown taking part in the hunt, and also outside his tent, surrounded by his suite, as he receives the kneeling Fieramonte. In several of the paintings ladies appear on a balcony or between the battlements of a wall.

Similar in style, though he paints more conventional scenes, is the illuminator of another chivalric romance, *Lancelot du Lac*. This master worked in the manner of Giovannino and Salomone de'Grassi. He has been identified with the anonymous illuminator of a Little Office in the Bibliothèque Nationale, Paris (MS. lat. 757), since the two codices show the same acute feeling for colour, narrative vein and close observation of reality. The Little Office in Paris is one of the most splendid Lombard codices because of its many full page illustrations, the richness of the decoration, the magnificence of the gold and the harmony of the colours. To the same master are attributed some of the illustrations in the *Tacuinum Sanitatis* (Bibliothèque Nationale, Paris; Nouv. Acq. lat. 1673). Other artists (their style is sometimes similar to that of

36    Guiron le Courtois. Nouv. Acq. fr. 5243. Lombard.
*Conversation between Knights.* Bibliothèque Nationale,
Paris.

36  Guiron le Courtois. Nouv. Acq. fr. 5243. Lombard. *Conversation between Knights*. Bibliothèque Nationale, Paris. A perceptive view of court life. Everything is in Lombard style, precisely observed: the clothes, the attitudes, the short ermine tunic of the principal personage, the group led by a man holding a torch, and the ladies who lean inquisitively from a loggia.

37  *Tristan*. MS. fr. 755. Lombard. *Hunting with a Falcon*. Bibliothèque Nationale, Paris. This is also a lively representation of an aspect of court life. The lines of the drawing are more conventional than in the previous example, but the pack of dogs barking as they set out on the hunt is full of life and movement.

38  *Tacuinum Sanitatis*. MS. Series Nova, 2644. Lombard in the manner of the de'Grassi. *The East Wind*. Österreichische Nationalbibliothek, Vienna. A little genre scene full of *brio*: the lady caught in the rain has covered her head with the edge of her cloak. The east wind, the caption explains, does no harm if it is accompanied by rain.

**37** *Tristan*. MS. fr. 755. Lombard. *Hunting with the Falcon*. Bibliothèque Nationale, Paris.

## Ventus orientalis.

Ventus oriental. oplo tpate cal. in 2. Electo transies p prata 7 loca pluuiosa. uuauitur mlti
plicat spē. Accumtiu nocer obtalmie. 7 cōre. Remōcium aqua flozi. gueit tpatis omi
etati. in uere. orientali regioī.

**38** *Tacuinum Sanitatis*. MS. Series Nova, 2644. Lombard,
in the manner of the de'Grassi. *The East Wind*. Oster-
reichische Nationalbibliothek, Vienna.

de'Grassi) collaborated in this work, which nonetheless has a certain stylistic unity. Here the Master of Lancelot indulges his taste for anecdote, introducing many animated figures like the tailor examining a lady's sleeve in plate 39. Closer to the manner of Porrino de'Grassi, according to Salmi, is the illustration of the *Tacuinum* in the Austrian National Library (plate 38), which shows the same *brio* and the same taste for anecdote.

Giovannino de'Grassi was one of the most gifted Lombard illuminators. He was a painter, sculptor and architect, and his name appears in 1389 in the *Annals* of the building of Milan Cathedral. His love for architecture appears in his illuminated work, in the motifs – spires, pinnacles, little chapels – he used. His passion for recording reality directly can be seen in the *Tacuino di Disegni* in the Biblioteca Civica, Bergamo, (MS. D.VII. 14), which includes studies of animals (stags and leopards, dogs, horses, bears, monkeys) in various attitudes, musicians, groups of ladies wearing the characteristically extravagant clothes of the period, and so on. The profusion of figures and animals, the splendid architectural motifs and the exuberant and fantastic decorative elements, reappear in the *Little Office of Gian Galeazzo Visconti*. Giovannino began the work in 1370 or 1380 (if the almost illegible date on one of the first illuminations is correct), but it was interrupted by his death in 1398. It was continued by his son Salomone, and later at the command of Filippo Maria Visconti, by Belbello da

Pavia. The codex is now in two parts: the part illuminated by Giovannino, now the property of the Duke
Visconti di Modrone; and a second part belonging to
the Landau Finaly Collection (no.22) now in the
Biblioteca Nazionale, Florence. In this part too,
the joint work of Giovannino and his son can occasionally be identified. The figures have a certain softness
of modelling, the colours are pale like those in the
*Tacuino* at Bergamo, and the invention is inex-
haustible: one page (plate 42) mainly taken up with a
large initial D also includes God the Father, and
spires, pinnacles and little chapels among the fronds
of the branches forming the initial and decorating the
margins.

The same type of illumination is found in the
*Breviarum Ambrosianum* in the Biblioteca Trivulziana, Milan, (MS. 2262), which also contains the
*Treatise of Beroldo* (sec. XII), about the customs of
the church in Milan. The breviary was illustrated by
Giovannino in collaboration with his sons. The first
page is illustrated with copious decoration and many
separate narratives with figures. In the lower margin
to the left is a representation of St Ambrose, who is
baptising St Augustine in the atrium of a Gothic
church with cusps and pinnacles; there is a highly
ornate spire in the right-hand margin like the
fantastic designs Giovannino made for the spires of
Milan Cathedral; and in the centre David is killing
Goliath (plate 43).

The manner of Giovannino is found in many other

codices executed during these years; he himself evidently worked on some of them, though always in collaboration with his brother Porrino and his son Salomone. The works are outstanding, in parts, and in some of them the master's style is interpreted in an original spirit.

The anonymous illuminator of the *Book of Hours of Isabella of Castile* (Royal Library, The Hague; MS. 76. F.6) must also be mentioned. He often employs the same elements as Giovannino – elegant figures moving like dancers, animals, architectural motifs – but with more delicacy of design and more clearly defined colours; and the narration proceeds without the impetus given by the master. However, some of the decoration is agreeably original. The decoration in plate 44, for example, consists entirely of two leafy trees whose trunks run along the side margins, their branches filling the top of the page with green; small children, birds and animals climb up the trunks or run along the ground or sit among the branches. To this illuminator can be attributed other codices in which the same delicate work appears, including the Book of Hours in the Biblioteca Estense, Modena, (R.7.3), which is perhaps the most closely related to the codex in the Hague.

Somewhat inferior to the art of Giovannino was that of Anovela da Imbonate. They share some traits, particularly the rendering of contemporary clothing and the delicate shading of the colours, although in Anovelo's work these sometimes clash violently. There

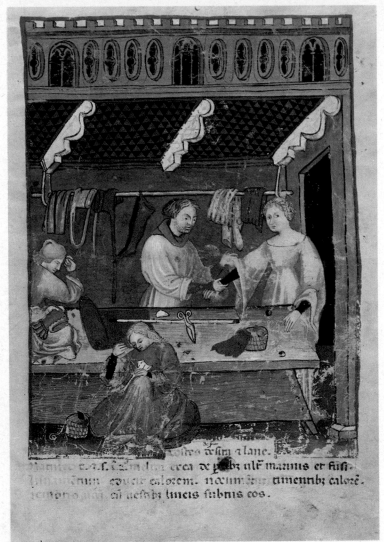

Citrn.

ıo. natııre. f. i.ʒ̇. f. ın. ʒ̇. melıoz ev eıs mꞁazes et ozꝛꝰfeꞇ. ıınamentım. flızın colleꝛıco, nocumentım. tꝛꝛbꝛnt ꝺıꝗꝛꝰ ſhonem. remotıo nonmenn. cum fıno melıs.

39  *Tacuinum Sanitatis*. Nouv. Acq. lat. 1673. The Master of Lancelot. *Tailor's Shop*. Bibliothèque Nationale, Paris. The interior of the shop is very effectively drawn. The tailor is taking the measurements of a lady client; the two workers are intent on their sewing.

40  *Tacuinum Sanitatis*. Nouv. Acq. lat. 1673. The Master of Lancelot. *Gathering Oranges*. Bibliothèque Nationale, Paris. The immediacy and freshness which characterise the preceding scene can be found again in this elegant portrayal of a man and woman gathering oranges.

41  Missal. MS. 6. Anovela da Imbonate. *The Coronation of Gian Galeazzo Visconti*. Biblioteca di S. Ambrogio, Milan. The ceremony unfolds in composed liturgical fashion. Above is the courtly procession; below, the crowning of the Duke.

41  Missal. MS. 6. Anovela da Imbonate. *The Coronation of Gian Galeazzo Visconti*. Biblioteca di S. Ambrogio, Milan.

are two missals by him in Milan, one in the Library of the church of S. Ambrogio (MS. 6), the other in the Library of Milan Cathedral (MS. II. D. 2). The first contains some pages at the beginning and end of the volume which show the coronation of Gian Galeazzo in S. Ambrogio in 1395 (plate 41), a genealogical table of the Visconti family, and various liturgical regulations. The missal was made by order of Gian Galeazzo, who gave it to the church in which he was crowned. Anovela illuminated some initial letters with figures, in one of which he signed his name, and two full pages. One of them is of the coronation ceremony, a page with splendid decoration and designs: leaf and flower motifs, zoomorphic images and Visconti enterprises are harmoniously combined, and the colours are brilliant and varied. The parts with figures, however, display certain characteristic weaknesses: the squatness of some of the people, the disproportion between their size and that of the chief figures, and the overcrowding of the scenes which makes them rather wearying to look at.

Michelino da Besozzo was a subtle and sensitive painter; the *Mystical Marriage of St Catherine*, in the Siena Pinacoteca, is his most characteristic work, demonstrating his extremely refined drawing and use of colour, and his close connection with the International Gothic style. His activity is recorded for the first time in Pavia in 1388, and in 1404 he was at work on the fabric of Milan Cathedral in succession to Giovannino de'Grassi. He is believed to be the illuminator of some codices which have obvious connections with the *Mystical Marriage*; the attribution is supported by the pictorial style of the illuminations, which are treated in the manner of easel paintings.

In the *Funeral Oration for Gian Galeazzo* by Father Pietro da Castellato (Bibliothèque Nationale, Paris; MS. lat. 5888) Gian Galeazzo is shown kneeling before the Virgin and Child surrounded by the Virtues, who possess the same childlike grace as St Catherine. Besozzo's delicate, sinuous and insubstantial figures also occur in a charming and intimate *Nativity* in a Book of Hours in the Bibliothèque Municipale at Avignon (MS.111), and in other illuminated work in the same codex. *The Trinity*, for example, represented by an unusual iconography sometimes found in 15th-century work, is a perfectly balanced composition combining sweetness with an almost severe gravity.

An illuminator known as the Master of the *Vitae Imperatorum* (his best-known work is the illustration of Suetonius' text) derives from Giovannino de'Grassi but shows a certain affinity with the style of Michelino; he is mentioned here only because of his derivation from artists who were still working in the full Gothic style. It is known that he was an Olivetan monk and produced a vast amount of work; his style became part of International Gothic and influenced Belbello da Pavia, who charged it with his Renaissance violence.

## The Neapolitan School

In Naples, to an even greater extent than in Lombardy, illumination was a splendid courtly art. The influence of French Gothic was very strong, since there were frequent contacts between the Anjou courts in Naples and France. Illuminations of a very high standard had been produced as early as the reign of Frederick II; but the efflorescence of the art occurred under the Angevins – most of all under Robert of Anjou (1309-1343), who liked to surround himself with artists and men of letters. Giotto went to Naples and painted many frescos, though none have survived. Simone Martini also worked there, and an altar by him showing the coronation of King Robert, has survived. A school of scribes and illuminators flourished at the court, and there is ample evidence that it also continued after Robert's death.

The *Book of Hours of Queen Joanna* (Austrian National Library; MS. 1921) is one of the outstanding examples of 14th-century Neapolitan illumination. Artists from Siena, Florence, France and Lombardy collaborated on it, and there are also some indications of Bolognese influence; and yet all the various influences are somehow blended – here, and in other works – into a specifically Neapolitan manner. The codex in which this is most clearly seen is the *Statute of the Order of the Holy Spirit*, now in the Bibliothèque Nationale in Paris (MS. fr. 4274). (The Order was a chivalric order founded by Louis of Tarentum and active between 1352 and 1362).

Work in similar style can be found in the *Hamilton Bible* in the Berlin Print Room; a Bible in the Vatican Library (lat. 3550); a Franciscan breviary in the National Library of Madrid (N.C.687); *King Meliadus*, a chivalric romance, and a *Divine Comedy*, both in the British Museum; and in several other codices. The figures often give an impression of impatient movement, and there is no attempt at characterisation; but the colours are resplendent golds, turquoises and reds (the backgrounds are turquoise and gold), and the decoration in the margins consists of stems, with rather stylised foliage in the Tuscan manner, among which appear birds and animals, and sometimes *drôleries* in the French or Bolognese style.

This decorative method had already appeared in Vincent de Beauvais' *Speculum Historiale*, illuminated by Filippo de Haya, King Robert's chancellor and Abbot of Cava in 1320. The work was certainly carried out in the scriptorium of the Abbey, where it is still kept (MS.26). The illuminations in this codex are of higher quality than those in the group described above; a particularly fine example is the large painting of nine kings in council, at the beginning of the second volume (plate 46). The strength of the modelling and the dignity with which the scene is rendered make it extremely impressive. In addition to French or English influences, reminiscences of the Bolognese manner are discernible in the arrangement of the figures and the way they are placed within the edifice surmounted by little turrets.

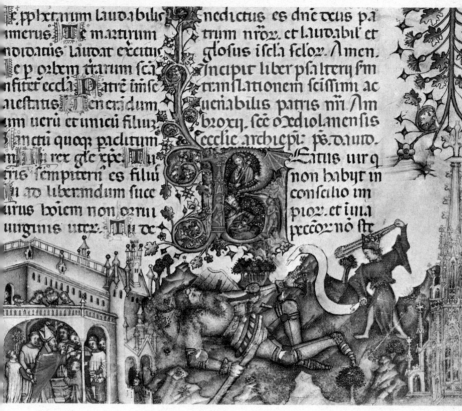

42   Little Office of the Visconti family. MS. Landau Finaly 22.
Giovaninno and Salomone de'Grassi. Capital letter: *God
giving His Blessing.* Biblioteca Nazionale, Florence. A fantastic
ensemble of flowers, little chapels, hills, clouds, hermits
resting beneath the trees which extend along the margins;
the whole dominated by the capital letter with God and
Angels; the illuminator's religiosity evidently leaned towards
the fabulous.

43   *Breviarum Ambrosianum.* MS. 2262. Giovannino de'
Grassi. *David and Goliath.* Biblioteca Trivulziana, Milan. The
central episode demonstrates very clearly the great Gothic
illuminator's gift for painting scenes of violence and intense
pathos.

44   *Book of Hours of Isabella of Castile.* MS. 76 F.6. School of
Giovannino de'Grassi. *Decorative motifs.* Koninkliste Bibliotheek, The Hague. This page is not of great interest from the
figurative point of view but its exuberant decorative fantasy
make it stand out from the rest of the codex.

45   Book of Hours MS. 111. Michelino da Besozzo. *The
Trinity* Bibliothèque Municipale, Avignon. Besozzo's delicate
art achieves unusual power in this Trinity. The iconography is
of an uncommon type.

44 *Book of Hours of Isabella of Castile*. MS. 76 F.6. School of Giovannino de'Grassi. *Decorative motifs*. Koninkliste Bibliotheek, The Hague.

**45**  Book of Hours MS. 111. Michelino da Besozzo. *The Trinity*. Bibliothèque Municipale, Avignon.

It was probably a Neapolitan artist directly acquainted with the Siena-Avignon style who illustrated a codex in the Biblioteca Nazionale in Naples (MS. V.A.16). The manner is more obviously courtly and the quality is quite high. It is an isolated work in Neapolitan production, and some critics doubt whether it really is connected with this school. The codex contains Boethius's treatises on arithemetic and music and other treatises on music. On one particularly beautiful page (plate 47), Music is represented as a charming and delicate female figure wearing a laurel crown. She is seated on a large throne, playing the organ, and is surrounded by figures playing instruments. Their attitudes are rhythmic, the colours warm, the drapery soft. At the top of the page, David is playing the psaltery; his figure is differently rendered from the others, being more comparable to those of the kings in the Cava Abbey codex.

Under the last Angevin kings artistic and cultural activity in Naples declined, and little of importance was produced until the reign of Alfonso of Aragon (1435-1458), when the Renaissance style held the field.


FRANCE

The 'Gothic line' began to appear in various parts of Europe at about the same time; but there is no doubt that Gothic architecture began in France with

the building of the Abbey of St Denis (begun in 1135).
It was commissioned by the Abbot of St Denis,
Suger, who was Louis VII's minister and Regent of
France during the Second Crusade. In one of his
writings Suger explains the essence of the new style of
building, describing how it was possible – thanks to
new processes of construction – to make walls less
massive and leave wide openings for windows, to let
more light into the interior. As a result, frescos began
to appear on the walls of churches, and the art of
stained glass came into being. This art also influenced
book illustrators, and in the first half of the following
century they were already decorating pages in a
manner suggested by stained glass. In the *Paris
Psalter* (Bibliothèque de l'Arsenal, MS. 1186), also
called the *Psalter of Blanche of Castile*, for example,
the scenes are arranged in medallions, two on each
page, exactly like those used in the oldest stained-glass
windows. The same arrangement is found in some
examples of a *Bible Moralisée* composed during the
reign of St Louis; fragments are preserved today in
various libraries of Europe and America. In the
example at the Bibliothèque Nationale in Paris
(MS. lat. 11560) the similarity of the large illuminated
pages to stained-glass windows is even more obvious
(plate 48). Each page contains eight scenes painted in
medallions, arranged in a double row: to the left
the Biblical narrative with a brief written commentary
next to it; to the right, the moral and the commentary.
The Gothic character of the figures and mode of

composition has begun to be apparent, and the similarity to stained glass is accentuated by the strong, clear-cut design, and the warmth of the colouring; the figures stand out against luminous gold backgrounds which might almost be letting in light.

French Gothic art really seems to take wing in the *Psalter of St Louis* (Bibliothèque Nationale, Paris; MS. lat. 10525), which is contemporary with or slightly later than the *Bible Moralisée*. The psalter proper is preceded by seventy-eight full-page Old Testament scenes. These are framed with Gothic arches, and their background is always the same: the Ste Chapelle in Paris, which was being built at the time. The slender, elongated figures are idealised and insubstantial, their faces are little more than outlines, and they express themselves by rhythmic movements and slight turns of the head; the thin, harmonious colours stand out against the rich gold of the background (plate 49).

From this point the aristocratic character of French illumination became increasingly apparent. The cultural centres of France were no longer the abbeys but the universities, especially the University of Paris; and they were closely connected with the Court. Louis IX and subsequent French sovereigns had their own libraries which entailed an increased demand for the services of scribes and illuminators, and effected an important shift in taste. Religious and liturgical works no longer predominated, and in any case now included many works of private devotion –

46 Vincent de Beauvais, *Speculum historiale*. MS. 26.
Neapolitan. *Assembly of Nine Kings*. Cava de'Tirreni, Abbey
Archives.

**47** Boethius, *De Musica, De Arithmetica*. MS. V.A. 14. Neapolitan. *Music and her votaries*. Biblioteca Nazionale, Naples.

46 Vincent de Beauvais, *Speculum historiale*. MS. 26. Neapolitan. *Assembly of Nine Kings*. Cava de'Tirreni, Abbey Archives. The strength and dignity of the kings, with their well-defined features, are comparable to certain characteristic English Gothic figures.

47 Boethius, *De Musica, de Arithmetica*. MS. V.A. 14. Neapolitan. *Music and her votaries*. Biblioteca Nazionale, Naples. The harmony of this composition, the warm tonal impasto, the grace of these well-constructed figures (especially the central one, Music) make this page a particularly outstanding example of Neapolitan work under the Angevins.

48 *Bible Moralisée*, said to be that of St Louis. MS. lat. 11560. French. 13th century. *The Last Judgement: the Chosen and the Condemned*. Bibliothèque Nationale, Paris. A series of eight medallions, each containing an episode from the Bible on blue and gold backgrounds; these pages are similar to the great stained-glass windows which at this period began to appear in French churches.

49 *Psalter of St Louis*. MS. lat. 10525. French, 13th century. *Stories of Rebecca*. Bibliothèque Nationale, Paris. The slender elongated figures moving with dance-like rhythms, the strongly-drawn faces and the pale colours which stand out against gold backgrounds signify the beginning of French Gothic illumination.

48 *Bible Moralisée*, said to be that of St Louis. MS. lat. 11560. French, 13th century. *The Last Judgment: the Chosen and the Condemned*. Bibliothèque Nationale, Paris.

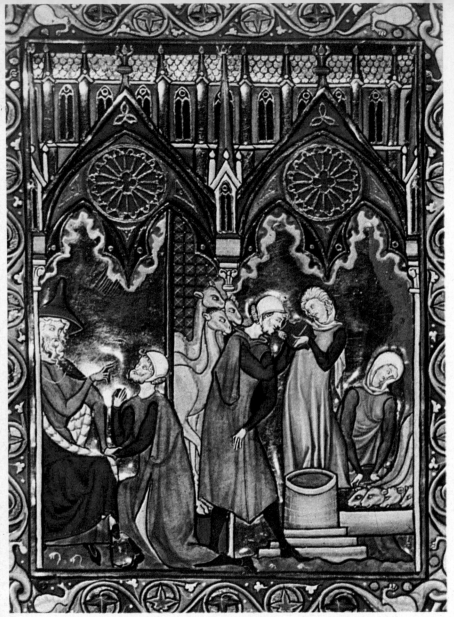

**49** *Psalter of St Louis*. MS. lat. 10525. French, 13th century. *Stories of Rebecca*. Bibliothèque Nationale, Paris.

offices and psalters for the royal family and leading
figures at court. As in the Italian courts, there were
many romances and chivalric poems, songs and works
of history. In general, the illuminators were no longer
clerics, but laymen who had their workshops in Paris.
The best-known of these masters was a certain
Honoré, who is often mentioned in documents. He
was probably active from about 1270, and had a
studio in the Rue Boutebrie. It is known that he sold a
codex of Gratian's *Decretum* in 1284, and that he
illuminated the *Breviary of Philippe le Bel*. This
breviary, now in the Bibliothèque Nationale, Paris
(MS. lat 1023), is one of the master's most important
codices; the full-page miniature at the beginning of
the text is his greatest achievement. The same manner
recurs in the many historiated initial letters, not all
of them perhaps from the hand of the master. The
decoration of the margins is interesting, being extremely simple and consisting of light branches,
taut and bare, which embrace the two columns of
the text, in some places also starting from the space
between them; a few sparse and stylised oak-leaves
grow from the branches. Many manuscripts were
produced by the school of Honoré, which was
carried on by the studio of Richard of Verdun and
continued until the first decades of the 14th century.
Its style was also assimilated by the illuminators
working outside the school, and even outside Paris,
with the result that it is not easy to distinguish between manuscripts illuminated by the master and

those disciples or imitators, who sometimes produced rather mannered work.

Breviaries and Books of Hours, stories of the saints and chivalric romances: in a courtly and highly idealised form they depict the life of Paris, at court and in the streets, life in the fields, hunting, battles, tournaments and banquets. In the *Breviary of Marguerite of Bar* (Bibliothèque Municipale, Verdun, MS. 107), attributed to an artist working in the north of France, some pages are decorated with designs rather similar to those in the Breviary of *Philippe le Bel*. They are, however, enlivened with playful, sometimes satirical figures, for example the scene showing a castle defended by rabbits and attacked by dogs armed with lances and spears while a dog wearing a crown waits in a tent. A French translation of the treatise on falconry attributed to Frederick II (Bibliothèque Nationale, Paris; MS. fr. 12400) was illuminated by one Simone d'Orléans. The illustrations – falcons, birds, stag-hunting with hounds and horses – occur almost exclusively in the margins, and in the lower margin especially the animals are represented with great naturalism.

The tendency to concentrate the decoration in the lower margin is found in many other codices. An illuminator fairly close to the school of Honoré illustrated a song-book (Bibliothèque de la Faculté de Médecine, Montepellier; MS. 196) in which the most animated and attractive of illuminations are painted in the lower margins. Here the illuminator had more space in which to develop his ideas (plate 50). The design is precisely drawn, the colouring is warm, the scenes are cheerful and harmonious, as befits a book of songs. In an initial letter, for example, there is a spring-time scene imbued with the spirit of chivalric and courtly literature: a young man has given a flower to a young woman under a tree while a knight riding by stops to observe the scene (plate 51). The charm of the picture lies in the lady's attitude, almost that of a dancer, and in the gesture with which the young man points to the gift. This gaiety, movement and balance is most often found in the scenes in the lower margins, where the figures often appear to be moving rhythmically.

Honoré's studio continued to produce extremely successful works; an *Histoire du Graal* by Robert de Borron (Bibliothèque Nationale, Paris; MS. fr. 95), a *Roman de Godefroi de Bouillon* (plate 52), also in the Bibliothèque Nationale (MS. fr. 22495), and a few examples of the *Biblia Historialis*. Among the most interesting works from the point of view of composition and iconography is a *Life of St Denis* (Bibliothèque Nationale; MS. fr. 2091) completed in 1317 (plate 53). The full-page illustrations recount episodes in the life of the saint in Paris, which is surrounded with walls, gates and towers. Each picture is framed in an architectural border with high pinnacles. The principal episode, often crowded with figures, occupies the centre of the composition, but the life of Paris goes on around it. Through the streets ride

**50** *Songs of Paris*. MS. 196. French. *Dances in a garden*.
Bibliothèque de la Faculté de Médecine, Montpellier.

50 *Songs of Paris*. MS. 196. French. *Dances in a garden.* Bibliothèque de la Faculté de Médecine, Montpellier, The scene in the lower margin is a gay commentary on the words of the song; its merits are its graceful movement and the harmony of the colour.

51 *Songs of Paris*. MS. 196. French. *Meeting of Two Lovers*. Bibliothèque de la Faculté de Médecine, Montpellier. The meeting of two lovers beneath a flowering tree has a slightly pathetic air. The freedom of the lines and the delicacy of the modelling are the salient features of this beautiful work.

52 *Roman de Godefroi de Bouillon*. MS. fr. 22495. Studio of Honoré's successors. *The King Giving Orders to a Group of Knights*. Bibliothèque Nationale, Paris. Honoré's style is employed unimaginatively in the drawing but with vivid colour. The large pages of this codex, on which the scenes form a sequence and the figures stand out clearly against brightly-coloured backgrounds, resemble enamel-work.

53 Yves, *Vie de St Denis*. MS. fr. 2091. Studio of Honoré's successors. *Episode from the life of St Denis*. Bibliothèque Nationale, Paris. The artist's lively narrative vein leads him to surround the episode of St Denis preaching with scenes of Parisian life. The people of Paris are transformed into stylised figures rendered with Gothic harmony of line and colour.

52   *Roman de Godefroi de Bouillon*. MS. fr. 22495.
Studio of Honoré's successors. *The King Giving Orders to a
Group of Knights*. Bibliothèque Nationale, Paris.

muñus

iracunt s. dyonis?

per fidei merita prebetur celica uita.

iam xpm creto iam disaplin s med

lisbius

knights or huntsmen with falcons; a street-vendor pushes a barrow heaped with his wares; workshops stand open to the street, showing workers of different types intent on their jobs. Below runs the Seine, along which boats pass with musicians, fishermen or merchandise. This demonstrates that at the beginning of the 14th century the life of the petit-bourgeoisie was arousing as much interest as court and religious life.

In the first decades of this century another illuminator was active in Paris who must have enjoyed considerable fame; this was Jean Pucelle, whose name first occurs in the breviary named after the Belleville family, to whom it belonged and for whom it was illuminated soon after 1323; it is now in the Bibliothèque Nationale, Paris (MS. lat. 10484). Pucelle's name appears here as the head of a studio which had probably been active for some time.

The work in which this master's qualities as an illustrator appear at their best is the *Book of Hours of Jeanne d'Evreux*, now in the Metropolitan Museum of Art (The Cloisters), New York. The artist adopted a technique which was to have outstanding success in France: monochrome illumination enhanced only with a few touches of gold and faint colouring. Since this was a work destined for a queen – Jeanne d'Evreux was the wife of Charles IV – the master himself probably executed it, whereas in the other works bearing his name students collaborated with him, for their names are added after his signature. The *Book of Hours* therefore makes it possible to

53    Yves, *Vie de St Denis*. MS. fr. 2091. Studio of Honoré's successors. *Episode from the life of St Denis*. Bibliothèque Nationale, Paris.

identify the individual characteristics of this master. His composition is not essentially different from that of Honoré, apart from his more rhythmical quality; but the strength of the modelling and the greater characterisation make it likely that Pucelle's work reflects the first reaction of French art to Italian models. The *Belleville Breviary* is illuminated on practically every page. Many pages are framed by a decorative border consisting of a narrow blue and gold stele which is broadened in some places by the addition of branches and stylised flowers; the branches bear the characteristically spiky leaves of Gothic ornamentation and sometimes carry grotesque little figures – animals with human heads, and birds and butterflies with delightful colours. This decoration runs around the page and also between the two columns of text. The illustrations are of incidents from the Bible or the stories of saints. They are sometimes placed within large initial letters, but more often in free panels of column width, and over a wider area at the bottom of the page; the latter sometimes continue the narrative in the square above, but more often refer to another Biblical incident, or to an episode which constitutes a kind of moral commentary on it. One of these pages (plate 54) shows Saul seated on a throne in his palace, aiming his lance at the boy David; at the bottom of the page Cain is killing Abel beside a sacrificial altar; and in the continuation of the illustration a priest is celebrating Mass in a small church, raising the host – the symbol

**54** *The Belleville Breviary*. MS. lat. 10483-10484. Jean Pucelle. *Saul Attempting to Kill David*. Bibliothèque Nationale, Paris.

54 *The Belleville Breviary.* MS. lat. 10483-10484. Jean Pucelle. *Saul Attempting to Kill David.* Bibliothèque Nationale, Paris. A page of exemplary elegance; the effect of harmony is achieved by the thematic development of the narrative, the arrangement of the text — skilfully broken up by the blue and gold initials — and the delicate and fantastic marginal decoration.

55 *Vita Sancti Antoni Abbatis.* MS. Med. Pal. 143. French. *The Legend of Patras: the Temptation of St Anthony.* Biblioteca Laurenziana, Florence. This famous episode from the life of St Anthony provides the illuminator with an opportunity to paint a charming group of girls; their clothes and head-dresses are rendered in detail.

56 *Breviary of Charles V.* MS. lat. 1052. School of Jean Pucelle. *Genre scene.* Bibliothèque Nationale, Paris. One of the many examples of the page layout devised by Jean Pucelle. The figures are of great expressive power, perhaps to the detriment of the delicacy of the total effect.

57 *Bible of Jean de Cis.* MS. fr. 15397. School of the Maître aux Bouqueteaux. *Abraham separating from Lot.* Bibliothèque Nationale, Paris. The illuminator strives to render volume and space in a manner not found in earlier French production. However, he preserved the delicate harmony of tone and composition characteristic of French Gothic.

**55** *Vita Sancti Antoni Abbatis.* MS. Med. Pal. 143. French.
*The Legend of Patras: the Temptation of St Anthony.*
Biblioteca Laurenziana, Florence.

56 *Breviary of Charles V*. MS. lat. 1052. School of Jean
Pucelle. *Genre scene*. Bibliothèque Nationale, Paris.

Itendit ergo
abram. et ꝛⁱ:
Quant au p
mier il dit amsi. Donꝙ̃

abram sen monta de
egipte lui et sa femme
et toutes les choses q̃ il
auoient. auec lui. ⁊ loth

57    *Bible of Jean de Cis*. MS. fr. 15397. School of the
Maitre aux Boqueteaux. *Abraham separating from Lot*.
Bibliothèque Nationale, Paris.

of sacrifice – while facing him is the figure of Charity repelling Hatred and giving alms to some beggars. In spite of the subject, there is no drama about these people: only the figures of Saul and Cain express a certain violence. The figure of Charity is delicate and well-modelled; instead of driving Hatred away, she seems to be performing a dance with him. In the margins are drawings of birds and insects, a little monkey trying to capture a butterfly, a grotesque figure riding on the back of a monster and playing the bagpipes. The colours are delicate and harmonious and endow the page with a feeling of grace and gaiety. This page has been described in detail because it is typical of Jean Pucelle and his followers.

There are illustrations of a simpler type in the Bible called after Robert de Billyng, the English scribe who signed it (Bibliothèque Nationale, Paris; MS. lat. 11935). The decoration is similar to Honoré's work in the *Breviary of Philippe le Bel*. The initial letters embellished with figures are extremely refined in design and colouring, but this Bible, which carries the date 1327, would not have been attributed to Jean Pucelle and his collaborators if they had not signed it.

The *Belleville Breviary* was also taken as a model in various devotional books illustrated for members of the royal family. The *Breviary of Charles V* (Bibliothèque Nationale, Paris; MS. lat. 1052) is very similar indeed – so much so that parts of the codex could be mistaken for a literal transcription of the earlier work. The same episodes appear at the bottom of the page on which

Saul is shown aiming his lance at David; and the page with David's fight with Goliath is also similar (plate 56). Here too there are three episodes at the bottom linked with the fight: the suicide of Judas, an old man dying inside a building and receiving the extreme unction, and a painting of Wisdom. There are some differences in the drawing of the figures, which are less idealised and closer to reality. There are also similar pages in a codex of the *Life of St Louis* written by Joinville. Episodes from the crusade undertaken by Louis IX provide opportunities for the representation of battle scenes, for example one beneath the walls of Damascus – a scene of great power on which the dark, harmonious colouring confers a deep seriousness.

These codices bring us almost into the second half of the 14th century. Jean Pucelle continued to work in the same extremely graceful and precious manner, but his art remained superficial. In the meantime a new trend, closely connected with the personality of John the Good, began. A portrait of John by the painter Girard d'Orléans has survived; it is a strongly realistic work which almost certainly reflects the king's personal taste. The artist or school which illuminated the Bible that the King had ordered Jean de Cis to translate into French, adopted a style in direct opposition to that of Pucelle and his school. Formal elegance was set aside in an attempt to achieve a more accurate representation of reality, and figures were endowed with personality, expression and three-dimensional contours. Jean de Cis did not finish his translation of the Bible much before 1356, the year of the battle of Poitiers, in which the king was captured; his long captivity put an end to work on the codex, which remained incomplete. But the scenes which the master succeeded in finishing showed many outstanding qualities: strength of composition, sureness of line and observation of animals and nature. Groups of leafy trees and thickets are found here, and appear in all the works attributed to this anonymous illuminator; they constitute his trade-mark, and his being called the Maître aux Bouqueteaux. He was not much concerned with colour; as a result, many of his illuminations are in monochrome, a technique which had also been used by Pucelle. He portrays animals with especial care, as in the scene where Abraham separates from Lot. (This illustration is probably not by the master but by one of the artists who towards the end of the century continued his work and tried to finish the illustration of the Bible.) Some works attributable to the Maître aux Bouqueteaux are clearer examples of his style. The best and most typical are the illustrations for the complete works of Guillaume de Machaut (Bibliothèque Nationale, Paris; MS. fr. 1584). The scenes are in monochrome, relieved only with light touches of colour; they show – for the first time in France – a landscape background extending as far as the horizon. Although the perspective is not too accurate, these backgrounds reveal careful observation of nature. The figures in the fore-

58  Guillaume de Machaut, *Oeuvres*. MS. fr. 1586. School
of the Maître aux Bouqueteaux. *Exchange of Rings between
a Lady and her Lover*. Bibliothèque Nationale, Paris.

58    Guillaume de Machaut, *Oeuvres.* MS. fr. 1586. School of the Maître aux Bouqueteaux. *Exchange of Rings between a Lady and her Lover.* Bibliothèque Nationale, Paris. Extremely refined and acutely observed; the figures are made convincing by the detailed reproduction of contemporary clothing.

59    Guyart des Moulins, *Bible Historiale.* MS. fr. 159. The Master of 1402. *Scenes from the Life of Solomon.* Bibliothèque Nationale, Paris. The product of a Parisian school recognisable by certain lines and designs, which are constantly repeated. The brightness of the colouring and the naturalness of the movement suggest the influence of Flemish artists.

60    Guyart des Moulins, *Bible Historiale.* MS. fr. 159. The Master of 1402. *Susannah Bathing.* Bibliothèque Nationale, Paris. In this scene also, the salient features are the lively and harmonious play of colours and the careful placing of the figures.

61    Boccaccio, *Des claires et nobles femmes.* MS. fr. 598. The Master of 1402. *The Wife of Tarquinius.* Bibliothèque Nationale, Paris. This work was produced by the same school, if not by the same artist, as the preceding illumination, and displays the same splendid qualities of colouring and construction.

Cy commencent les paraboles salomo
en françois sur la bible et hystoire ❧
&s paraboles salomon le filz
de dauid roy dysrael ascauoir
sapience et discipline a en
tre paroles et prudence a
receuoir enseignemens
et doctrine et iustice et iu
gement et loyaulte et droiture que seus

terpretacions et les figures et les paroles
des sages. La parolle de nreseigneur est co
mencement de sapience les fols respriseur
sapience et doctrine mon filz oye la disci
pline de ton pere et ne laisse mie la loy de
ta mere que grace soit adioustee unte
sur ton chief et fermail dor a ton col mo
filz se les pecheurs taleichent ne les croy mie
C'est a dire se les losengiers te losengent

**59** Guyart des Moulins, *Bible Historiale*. MS. fr. 159. The
Master of 1402. *Scenes from the Life of Solomon*.
Bibliothèque Nationale, Paris.

**60** Guyart des Moulins, *Bible Historiale*. MS. fr. 159. The Master of 1402. *Susannah Bathing*. Bibliothèque Nationale, Paris.

61    Boccaccio, *Des claires et nobles femmes*. MS. fr. 598.
The Master of 1402. *The Wife of Tarquinius*. Bibliothèque
Nationale, Paris.

ground, usually allegorical, move very naturally; and wherever the author is represented we see a face so individual and expressive that it appears to be a true portrait. The people are all dressed in the affected and ornate clothes fashionable at the time.

The many other manuscripts attributed to this master, for example Charles V's copy of Livy, demonstrate that he had assimilated the influence of Italian illumination (which Pucelle too had felt but only superficially absorbed). The study of external reality, the volumes of the figures, the depth of the backgrounds and, not least, the attention to contemporary dress, are characteristic of Lombard art; but Gothic illumination in France always retained its delicacy of drawing, grace of gesture and tonal harmony. It is appropriate at this juncture to mention the delicate figures (plate 58) in another codex of the works of Guillaume de Machaut, also in the Bibliothèque Nationale (MS. fr. 1586), because of the wonderful grace of the figures, their self-confident smiling faces, and their clothes, represented with a scrupulous care worthy of fashion plates. French artists proved capable of assimilating (without merely copying) the ideas which towards the end of the century reached them from Italy and Flanders, taking whatever could be useful to their art without sacrificing their own qualities and characteristics. The strongest contact with Italy occurred via the Sienese illuminators working in Avignon; and some Flemish artists came to Paris. At the end of the century, for example, Jean de Bruges was at the court of Charles V; he was a painter and illuminator, and painted the king's portrait on the first page of a Bible. André Beauneveu was active at the same time in Paris, and although he was principally a painter, his manner appears on the pages of several manuscripts. He worked most for the Duc de Berry, a typical example of a humanist prince, a lover of art and fine books. It was probably Beauneveu who executed some of the figures in the psalter (Bibliothèque Nationale, Paris; MS. fr. 13091) said to have been carried out for the Duc de Berry. Jacquemart de Hesdin was also working in Paris at the same time; he carried on the style of Jean Pucelle into the early 15th century. Some authorities have credited him with the illustrations in the *Breviary of Charles V*; but his style and work have given rise to violent disagreements. Several of the many Books of Hours made for the Duc de Berry have been attributed to him, in particular the *Petites Heures* in the Bibliothèque Nationale (MS. lat. 18014). The work was executed in about 1390, and Jacquemart must have collaborated with André Beauneveu. It contains extremely delicate drawing, and although it shows a greater sense of volume, develops the decorative method already noted in the *Belleville Breviary*; this is especially noticeable in the calendar. The story of the Passion is rendered with an intensity of expression of which everything else indicates that this artist was incapable. For this reason, the most recent critical opinion excludes the possibility that Jacquemart illuminated *Les Très Belles Heures* in Brussels (Bibliothèque Royale; MS. 11060), which had been regarded by some authorities as a collaboration between him and Beauneveu. Today it is usually attributed to an anonymous illuminator influenced by the Sienese school, in particular by the works of Simone Martini and his pupils in Avignon.

These artists and codices bring us to the early 15th century, when art assumed the characteristics appropriately labelled 'International Gothic' (a period not possible to cover in this book), for they resulted from the interaction of various regional and national schools. One more artist – or school – must be included in this process of interaction: the Master of 1402. His most characteristic works are the *Bible Historiale* of Guyart des Moulins (plates 59 and 60) in the Bibliothèque Nationale (MS. fr. 159), and a copy of Boccaccio's *De Claris Mulieribus* translated into French (plate 61), also in the Bibliothèque Nationale (MS. fr. 598). They have several characteristics in common: their colouring, and a sense of space and movement which show the invigorating influence of Flemish art. The Bible preserves some traditional formal elements, such as the arrangement of the narrative within frames for each page (the layout used by Honoré) and the chequered gold and blue backgrounds. But in every scene there is a depth and natural movement which make the narrative both realistic and lively; and the colours of the clothing are bright and sometimes violent, but always harmonious.

**62** Cistercian psalter from the Diocese of Basel. MS. 54.
German, 13th century. *Annunciation, Visitation, Nativity*.
Bibliothèque Municipale, Besançon.

**63** *The Manesse Manuscript*. MS. Pal. germ. 848. *A Poet Offering his Book to a Lady*. University Library, Heidelberg.

Waz preys wil der peiagen

**64** Hugo von Trimberg, *Der Renner*. MS. V.u.74. German.
*Knight Attacking*. Royal Library, Stockholm.

62  Cistercian psalter from the Diocese of Basel. MS. 54. German, 13th century. *Annunciation, Visitation, Nativity.* Bibliothèque Municipale, Besançon. Through the skilful use of proportion the artist has been able to infuse his characters with an ingenious expressiveness in which Byzantine and Ottonian influences are discernible.

63  *The Manesse Manuscript.* MS. Pal. germ. 848. *A Poet Offering his Book to a Lady.* University Library, Heidelberg. The expression of a refined and conventional courtly art; but the composition is notably harmonious, as are the gestures by which the characters express their feelings.

64  Hugo von Trimberg, *Der Renner.* MS. V.u.74. German. *Knight Attacking.* Royal Library, Stockholm. The knight is stylised almost to the point of caricature, but he has been given great expressive power. Notice how his long sleeves are used to balance the composition.

65.  Stricker, *The History of Charlemagne.* MS. germ. 623. German. *Roland dying.* University Library, Tübingen. A typical scene of a legendary event, very Germanic in feeling and with a touch of caricature.

66  *The Book of Hours of Maria von Geldern.* MS. germ. 42. Rhenish. *Annunciation.* University Library, Tübingen. This slender figure of sophisticated refinement is set against a vermillion background: the iconography of the cherubim who make the Annunciation is unusual.

65　Stricker, *The History of Charlemagne*. MS. germ. 623.
German. *Roland dying*. University Library, Tübingen.

**66** *The Book of Hours of Maria von Geldern.* MS. germ. 42. Rhenish. *Annunciation.* University Library, Tübingen.

# GERMANY

Early Gothic illumination in Germany still contained some of the elements which had contributed to the formation of German Romanesque: reminiscences of Ottonian art of a strongly expressionistic type are mingled with Byzantine influences, though these remain formal and external, evident in a rigid, almost metallic line in the clothing, and in the accentuated calligraphic treatment of the drapery. The psalter from the Diocese of Basel (now in the Bibliothèque Municipale, Besançon: MS. 54) was executed in about 1260, and can be regarded as the bridge between the Romanesque and the Gothic (plate 62). The harmonious arrangement of the figures and the graceful attitudes are uneasily combined with expressive intensity and dramatic contours more reminiscent of certain Bolognese figures than the elegant idealisation of French Gothic.

Traces of the Romanesque style remain in German illuminated work throughout the 13th century, and only during the 14th did a new art, open to influences from France and Italy, come into being. The strength and direction of the influence varied from region to region, and there were also notable variations in the styles of illumination. Some of the figures produced by the Bohemian school are strongly expressionistic and influenced neighbouring areas. The Rhineland felt the influence of French Gothic more deeply than any other region, and Rhenish artists were best able to interpret its spirit. This can be seen in the delicate *Annuciation* in the *Wettingen Gradual* (Canton Library of Aarau), which is close to the Cologne school of painting; and in the splendid *Michael the Archangel Killing the Dragon* on a detached page (now in the Department of Prints and Drawings, Berlin) attributed to the same master. The grace of French Gothic is also found in the *Manesse Manuscript,* a collection of troubadours' songs called after the noble family of Manesse, who were responsible for the collection. The style of the master who illustrated this codex resembles that of the artists working round Lake Constance and in the neighbourhood of Zürich. The grace of the illustrations was perhaps inspired by the content of the songs; one of the most significant figures is that of the Minnesinger Heinrich von Verdecke in a mood of happy meditation. His head resting in the palm of his hand, he sits amid flowers and birds, the subjects of his songs. Other illustrations are colder and more static, like the one in which the poet offers his book to a lady (plate 63); the only expressive elements are the gestures of the hands and the delicate pose of the female figure. Another artist from the school of Lake Constance, comparable to the Master of the Manesse Manuscript, was the illuminator of a copy of the *History of Charlemagne* in the dialect of central Germany. There is a fragment of this work in the University Library of Tübingen (plate 65). The figure of the dying Roland displays the same inexpressive rigidity; his soul, strangely symbolised by his glove, is ascending to heaven and being received by God, while Roland strikes down a Saracen with his horn. The Master who illustrated the *Universal Chronicle* of Rudolph of Ems came from the same district but was a much better artist; in the illustrations for the story of Samson his figures have an unusual expressive vigour, as in the incident showing Samson, his long hair in disarray, fighting the lion.

## BOHEMIA

In the second half of the 14th century the Bohemian school was the most important; its influence was increased by the residence in Prague of the Emperor Charles IV, King of Bohemia, and his ministers. These included Johan von Neumarkt, who had known Petrarch in Italy and assimilated Humanist ideas. Bohemian manuscripts of the period were influenced by certain stylistic features of the Italian school, as is evident in a military treatise, Conrad von Eichstatt's *Bellifortis* (University Library of Göttingen), and the *Gospel Book of Albert III of Austria* (Austrian National Library; MS. 1182), done for Johan von Neumarkt by the scribe and illuminator Johan von

**67** *Queen Mary Psalter*. MS. Royal 2.B.VII. East Anglian school. *The Massacre of the Innocents*. British Museum, London.

**68** *The Peterborough Psalter*. MS. 53. East Anglian School. *Malachi and Simeon*.

67.   *Queen Mary Psalter.* MS. Royal 2.B.VII. East Anglian School. *The Massacre of the Innocents.* British Museum, London. At once extremely elegant and horrific; the king is the dramatic centre of this splendidly vigorous composition.

68   *The Peterborough Psalter.* MS. 53. East Anglian School. *Malachi and Simeon.* The two prophets facing each other are part of a larger rhythm which is prolonged in the volutes of the trilobal arches. The iconography is somewhat unusual.

69   Apocalypse. MS. 20. English school. *Enthronement of Christ.* Corpus Christi College, Cambridge. Christ triumphant, surrounded by his court like an Oriental sovereign, is majestic and awe-inspiring, a judge rather than a saviour. All the figures in this crowded scene — spilling over in places on to the border — participate intensely in the event.

**69** Apocalypse. MS. 20. English school. *Enthronement of Christ*. Corpus Christi College, Cambridge.

Troppaul. In spite of certain harsh elements, von Troppaul's style is elegant and refined. Although deriving from the Bohemian school, the illuminator of Hugo von Trimberg's short allegorical and didactic poem *The Corridor* worked in a rather original style. The illuminations were executed in about 1400 with bold lines and strongly expressive, extremely stylised figures. Some knights, represented almost as heraldic symbols, are particularly original (plate 64).

At the beginning of the 15th century, Germany adopted International Gothic. The graceful Annunciation (plate 66) in the *Book of Hours of Maria von Geldern* (University Library of Tübingen; MS. ger. 42) is a fine example. The iconography is unusual: the Virgin is represented not as *ancilla Domini* (handmaiden of the Lord), but as a queen receiving homage. She wears a rich azure *houppelande* lined with white, and stands firmly upright with a book in her hand. Flemish and French influences are blended to produce a work of delicate refinement; all religious feeling, however, has vanished.

## ENGLAND

Gothic illuminated work in England carried on the splendid ancient tradition. (In the centuries before AD 1000 work from Ireland and England had introduced highly elaborate and fanciful decorative motifs into the rest of Europe.) The first indications of the Gothic manner are visible in the grace, flexibility and freedom of the drapery on certain figures painted by the Salisbury Cathedral school towards the middle of the 13th century; elsewhere, for example at St Albans, the expressive vigour of Matthew Paris's work was still the norm.

Towards the end of the century, the East Anglian school began to be active. Its centre was in Peterborough, and it became at once the greatest and most characteristic of the English schools in this golden age of illumination. The expressiveness and dramatic power of these illuminators gave a highly individual tone to the sinuous and elegant Gothic figures and exuberant decoration.

The *Peterborough Psalter with Bestiary* (Corpus Christi College, Cambridge; MS. 53) includes Madonnas who possess the grace of their Sienese counterparts interpreted in English style, and slender, dignified figures of prophets (plate 68). The masterpiece of the East Anglian school is the *Queen Mary Psalter* (British Museum; Royal 2.B.VII), in which expressive intensity is combined with elegant and harmonious composition (plate 67).

Most English illumination was executed on psalters, missals and Bibles; but there was also a special type of manuscript, the 'Apocalypse', in which the narrative proceeds through the illustrations. In these – for example in the work reproduced in plate 69 – English illuminators were able to express their powerful individual quality, at once elevated and intensely dramatic.

# LIST OF ILLUSTRATIONS          Page